Collins Revised

Engaging English 5

Ruby Bose
Anju Gupta

Components of DigiSuite

Student + Teacher			Teacher-only	
a animations	**ia** activities	**g** games	**lp** lesson plans	**tn** teacher's notes
ilt instructor-led tutorials	**w** worksheets	**v** videos	**w** worksheets	**ak** answer keys
	audio			

Preface

Revised Engaging English aims to instill an appreciation for literature in today's learners, while equipping them with the tools to develop native fluency and communicative competence in using the English language.

This eight-level series has been designed to teach language skills through the use of literature. Comprising Coursebooks and Workbooks, and digital resources for teachers for all levels, the series is meant to be educative as well as inspiring, imparting moral values and arousing the learner's curiosity about the world beyond the classroom.

In the revised edition, the series has been aligned closely with the guidelines of the National Education Policy, 2020 through its focus on twenty-first century skills, Sustainable Development Goals (SDGs), cross-curricular learning, 'Happiness' content and art-integrated learning. Coursebooks 1 and 2 integrate the essence of NIPUN (National Initiative for Proficiency in Reading with Understanding and Numeracy), which deals with Foundational Literacy and Numeracy. They aim to motivate students to read independently, improve their vocabulary, develop their critical thinking and creative skills and enhance their ability to express themselves verbally and in writing.

The lessons are built around carefully selected literary pieces with distinct cross-curricular themes, and presented with glossary, explanation of literary terms and interesting trivia. The end-of-chapter exercises address the needs of formal language learning and cover all aspects of language acquisition. They include *Comprehension, Way with Words, Grammar in Use, Study Skills, Listening and Speaking* and *Pen it Down.*

New Features in the Revised Edition

Let's Get Started: A theme-based, cross-curricular warm-up task at the beginning of each lesson spanning subjects like science, history and general knowledge, with a focus on SDGs.

Graphic stories: These include both fiction and non-fiction and address the needs of visual learners.

Cross-curricular trivia: This includes **Did You Know?**, which has interesting information covering science, mathematics, geography, history and general knowledge, related to the passage.

In-text questions: These assess while-reading comprehension of the learner.

Life Skills and Values: A part of Comprehension, this includes questions that encourage learners to think analytically and write creatively, thus building higher order thinking skills. They are aligned to the twenty-first century skills.

Augmented scaffolding: This comprises more detailed explanations for every section, including Way with Words and Grammar in Use. Concepts are presented through graphic organizers and reinforced through practice and repetition. Support is provided for the Listening and Speaking and Pen it Down tasks in the form of suggested points as well as useful words and phrases to facilitate competency-based learning.

Now I can: This is a learner-centric self-assessment checklist of the learning objectives for every lesson.

Be Creative!/Research and Write: These special pages, of which there are three in each book, include several new research-based literary projects, creative writing and vocabulary tasks which revisit the themes of the lessons. These focus variously on art integration and SDGs and support inquiry-based learning.

The **Workbooks** complement the Coursebooks by providing additional skills practice through the careful mapping of grammar and vocabulary. Each Workbook from Classes 3 to 8 includes a test paper based on the principle of SAFAL (Structured Assessment For Analyzing Learning), a competency-based assessment introduced by CBSE in keeping with the guidelines of the NEP. They focus on assessing the competencies of critical thinking as well as inquiry-based and analysis-based learning.

The series is supported with **Teacher's Resource Books** and **Digital resources**.

The series encourages competency-based education which allows concept acquisition at the learner's own pace, based on individual ability. We hope that it will foster a love for literature and reading in young learners.

Authors

Ruby Bose has been teaching English for more than a decade at The Heritage School, Kolkata.
Anju Gupta is an ELT author and materials developer.

Key Features

Let's Get Started

- Theme-based warm-up activities, with a focus on Sustainable Development Goals

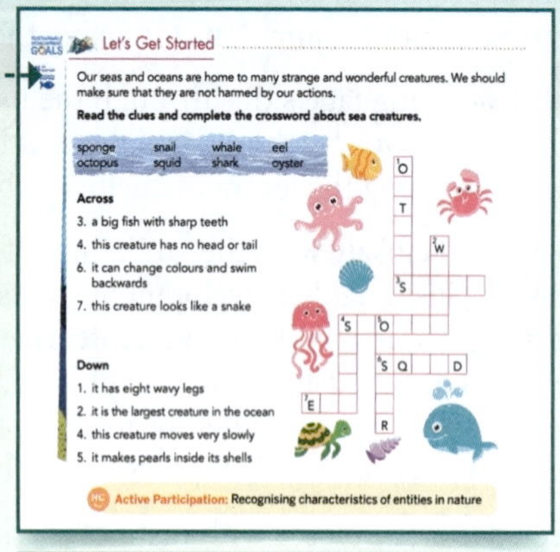
Let's Get Started

Our seas and oceans are home to many strange and wonderful creatures. We should make sure that they are not harmed by our actions.

Read the clues and complete the crossword about sea creatures.

sponge snail whale eel octopus squid shark oyster

Across

3. a big fish with sharp teeth
4. this creature has no head or tail
6. it can change colours and swim backwards
7. this creature looks like a snake

Down

1. it has eight wavy legs
2. it is the largest creature in the ocean
4. this creature moves very slowly
5. it makes pearls inside its shells

Active Participation: Recognising characteristics of entities in nature

Reading

- Has a rich variety of reading passages, including prose, poetry and drama
- Covers literary genres like short stories, biographies, folktales, fables, fantasy, science fiction, non-fiction, extracts from contemporary and classic works, taken from Indian and world literature

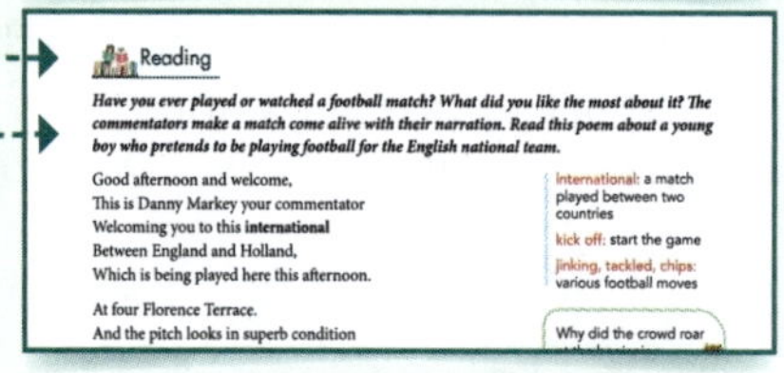
Reading

Have you ever played or watched a football match? What did you like the most about it? The commentators make a match come alive with their narration. Read this poem about a young boy who pretends to be playing football for the English national team.

Good afternoon and welcome,
This is Danny Markey your commentator
Welcoming you to this **international**
Between England and Holland,
Which is being played here this afternoon.

At four Florence Terrace.
And the pitch looks in superb condition

international: a match played between two countries
kick off: start the game
jinking, tackled, chips: various football moves

Why did the crowd roar

Introduction

- Includes background information about the reading text to initiate learners into the passage

Wordwise

- Provides additional information on the origin of words to interest learners in the nuances of language and to improve vocabulary

In-text questions

- 'while-reading' questions to check textual understanding

Wordwise

1. A toadstool is a type of mushroom that cannot be eaten. The name came from the belief that toads often sat on these mushrooms, which look like stools.

Under a toadstool[1]
Crept a **wee** elf,
Out of the rain,
To shelter himself.

Under the toadstool
Sound asleep,
Sat a big **dormouse**
All in a **heap**.

Trembled the wee elf,
Frightened, and yet
Fearing to fly away
Lest he get wet.

To the next shelter —
Maybe a mile!
Sudden the wee elf
Smiled a wee smile,

Tugged till the toadstool
Toppled in two.
Holding it over him,
Gaily he flew.

Soon he was safe home,
Dry as could be.
Soon woke the dormouse —
'Good gracious me!'

'Where is my toadstool?'
Loud he **lamented**.
And that's how umbrellas
First were **invented**.

crept: moved with the body close to the ground
wee: tiny
dormouse: a small, mouse-like animal with a furry tail
heap: untidily piled things
trembled: shook in fear
lest: in case
tugged: pulled
toppled: fell
gaily: happily
lamented: complained
invented: created

How far away was the next shelter?

About the author

Oliver Herford (1863–1935) was an American writer and artist. He was known for his funny writings. Some of his popular poems are 'The Chimpanzee' and 'The Hen'.

50

Comprehension

- 'Quick Recap' checks factual understanding through 'who', 'what', 'where', and 'how' questions; also includes 'reference to context' questions to test in-depth understanding of the lesson

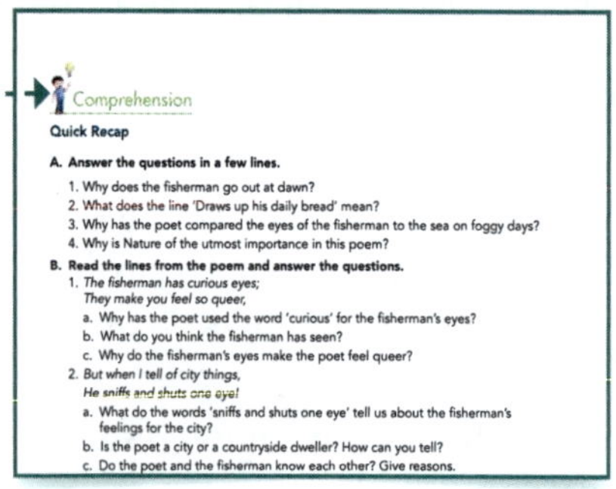
Comprehension

Quick Recap

A. Answer the questions in a few lines.

1. Why does the fisherman go out at dawn?
2. What does the line 'Draws up his daily bread' mean?
3. Why has the poet compared the eyes of the fisherman to the sea on foggy days?
4. Why is Nature of the utmost importance in this poem?

B. Read the lines from the poem and answer the questions.

1. *The fisherman has curious eyes;*
   They make you feel so queer,
   a. Why has the poet used the word 'curious' for the fisherman's eyes?
   b. What do you think the fisherman has seen?
   c. Why do the fisherman's eyes make the poet feel queer?
2. *But when I tell of city things,*
   He sniffs and shuts one eye!
   a. What do the words 'sniffs and shuts one eye' tell us about the fisherman's feelings for the city?
   b. Is the poet a city or a countryside dweller? How can you tell?
   c. Do the poet and the fisherman know each other? Give reasons.

Life Skills and Values

- Inferential and extrapolative higher order thinking skills (HOTS) questions on moral values and interpersonal skills, mapped to twenty-first century skills

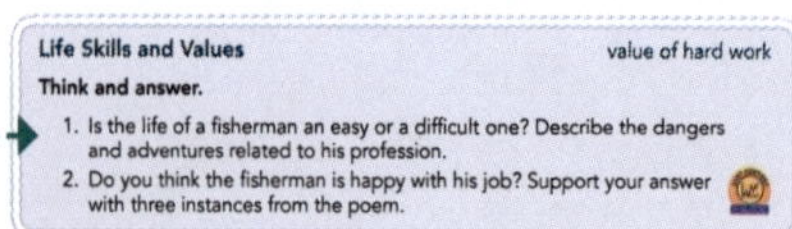
Life Skills and Values value of hard work

Think and answer.

1. Is the life of a fisherman an easy or a difficult one? Describe the dangers and adventures related to his profession.
2. Do you think the fisherman is happy with his job? Support your answer with three instances from the poem.

Graphic Story

- Graphic story in Classes 1-7 to aid visual learning

Glossary

- Provides contextual meanings of difficult words and phrases, given alongside the reading passage

About the author/poet

- Gives a brief biography of the writer, with names of their best known works

Literary term, Did You Know?

- Provide additional information on literary devices and figures of speech, and trivia to develop cross-curricular intelligence

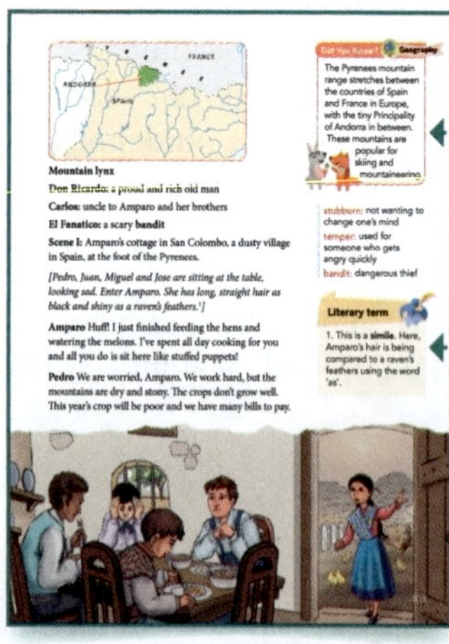
Did You Know? Geography

The Pyrenees mountain range stretches between the countries of Spain and France in Europe, with the tiny Principality of Andorra in between. These mountains are popular for skiing and mountaineering.

Mountain lynx
Don Ricardo: a proud and rich old man
Carlos: uncle to Amparo and her brothers
El Fanatico: a scary bandit
Scene I: Amparo's cottage in San Colombo, a dusty village in Spain, at the foot of the Pyrenees.

[Pedro, Juan, Miguel and Jose are sitting at the table, looking sad. Enter Amparo. She has long, straight hair as black and shiny as a raven's feathers.]

Amparo Huff! I just finished feeding the hens and watering the melons. I've spent all day cooking for you and all you do is sit here like stuffed puppets!

Pedro We are worried, Amparo. We work hard, but the mountains are dry and stony. The crops don't grow well. This year's crop will be poor and we have many bills to pay.

stubborn: not wanting to change one's mind
temper: used for someone who gets angry quickly
bandit: dangerous thief

Literary term

1. This is a **simile**. Here, Amparo's hair is being compared to a raven's feathers using the word 'as'.

Way with Words

- Includes exercises on contextual application of language encountered in the reading text
- Fosters appreciation of literary devices and figures of speech (simile, metaphor, personification, etc)

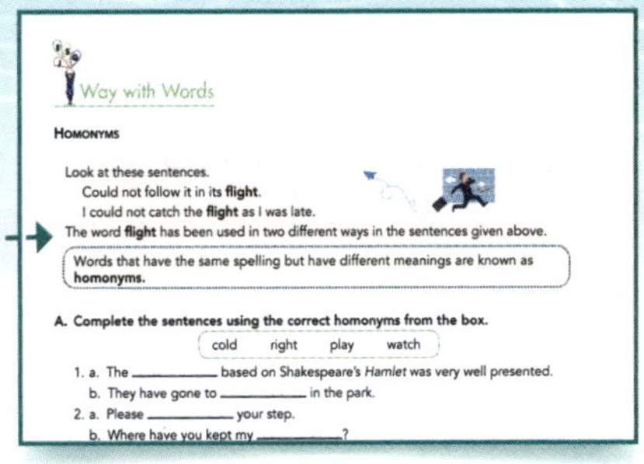

Way with Words

HOMONYMS

Look at these sentences.
Could not follow it in its **flight**.
I could not catch the **flight** as I was late.
The word **flight** has been used in two different ways in the sentences given above.

Words that have the same spelling but have different meanings are known as **homonyms**.

A. Complete the sentences using the correct homonyms from the box.

cold right play watch

1. a. The __________ based on Shakespeare's *Hamlet* was very well presented.
b. They have gone to __________ in the park.
2. a. Please __________ your step.
b. Where have you kept my __________?

Grammar in Use

- Imparts formal understanding of language structures and syntax
- Includes easy-to-understand explanations of grammar concepts, graphic organisers and plenty of practice exercises

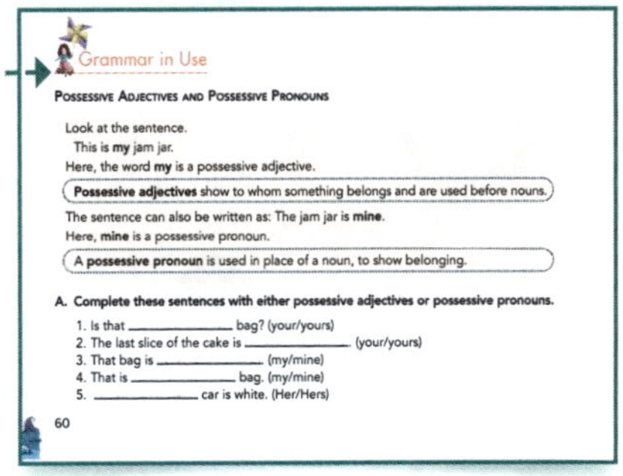

Grammar in Use

POSSESSIVE ADJECTIVES AND POSSESSIVE PRONOUNS

Look at the sentence.
This is **my** jam jar.
Here, the word **my** is a possessive adjective.

Possessive adjectives show to whom something belongs and are used before nouns.

The sentence can also be written as: The jam jar is **mine**.
Here, **mine** is a possessive pronoun.

A **possessive pronoun** is used in place of a noun, to show belonging.

A. Complete these sentences with either possessive adjectives or possessive pronouns.

1. Is that __________ bag? (your/yours)
2. The last slice of the cake is __________ (your/yours)
3. That bag is __________ (my/mine)
4. That is __________ bag. (my/mine)
5. __________ car is white. (Her/Hers)

60

Listening and Speaking

- Facilitates fluency in oral and aural communication
- Includes conversation practice, role plays, debates and listening comprehension
- Exercises on rhyme and meter in poetry chapters

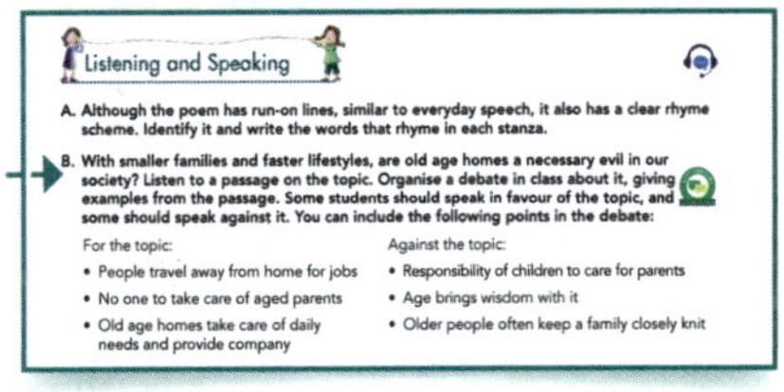

Listening and Speaking

A. Although the poem has run-on lines, similar to everyday speech, it also has a clear rhyme scheme. Identify it and write the words that rhyme in each stanza.

B. With smaller families and faster lifestyles, are old age homes a necessary evil in our society? Listen to a passage on the topic. Organise a debate in class about it, giving examples from the passage. Some students should speak in favour of the topic, and some should speak against it. You can include the following points in the debate:

For the topic:
- People travel away from home for jobs
- No one to take care of aged parents
- Old age homes take care of daily needs and provide company

Against the topic:
- Responsibility of children to care for parents
- Age brings wisdom with it
- Older people often keep a family closely knit

Pen it Down

- Includes guided and free writing tasks, to enable learners to express themselves creatively, logically and coherently

Now I can

- Self-assessment of learning objectives for the chapter

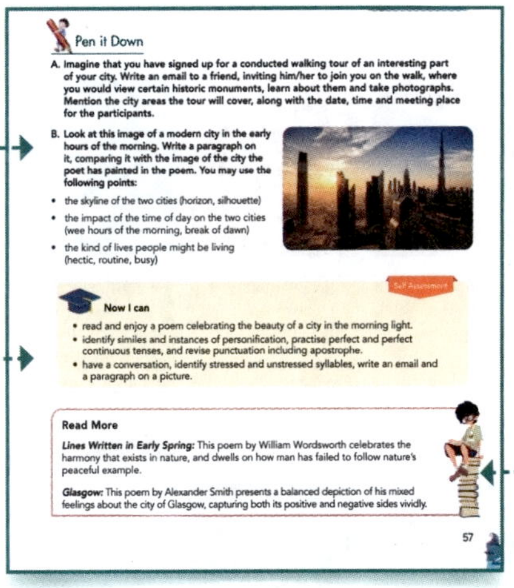

Pen it Down

A. Imagine that you have signed up for a conducted walking tour of an interesting part of your city. Write an email to a friend, inviting him/her to join you on the walk, where you would view certain historic monuments, learn about them and take photographs. Mention the city areas the tour will cover, along with the date, time and meeting place for the participants.

B. Look at this image of a modern city in the early hours of the morning. Write a paragraph on it, comparing it with the image of the city the poet has painted in the poem. You may use the following points:

- the skyline of the two cities (horizon, silhouette)
- the impact of the time of day on the two cities (wee hours of the morning, break of dawn)
- the kind of lives people might be living (hectic, routine, busy)

Self Assessment

Now I can
- read and enjoy a poem celebrating the beauty of a city in the morning light.
- identify similes and instances of personification, practise perfect and perfect continuous tenses, and revise punctuation including apostrophe.
- have a conversation, identify stressed and unstressed syllables, write an email and a paragraph on a picture.

Read More

Lines Written in Early Spring: This poem by William Wordsworth celebrates the harmony that exists in nature, and dwells on how man has failed to follow nature's peaceful example.

Glasgow: This poem by Alexander Smith presents a balanced depiction of his mixed feelings about the city of Glasgow, capturing both its positive and negative sides vividly.

57

Study Skills

- Develops the sub-skills of language study
- **Spell Check** and **Pronounce Well** include phonics drills and exercises on spelling
- **Use Your Dictionary** develops dictionary referencing skills

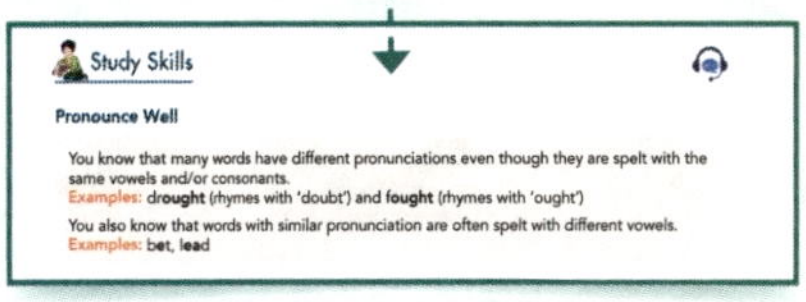

Study Skills

Pronounce Well

You know that many words have different pronunciations even though they are spelt with the same vowels and/or consonants.
Examples: **drought** (rhymes with 'doubt') and **fought** (rhymes with 'ought')
You also know that words with similar pronunciation are often spelt with different vowels.
Examples: **bet, lead**

Literary Genres and Terms

- Includes a glossary to introduce literary genres and explain literary devices and narrative tools

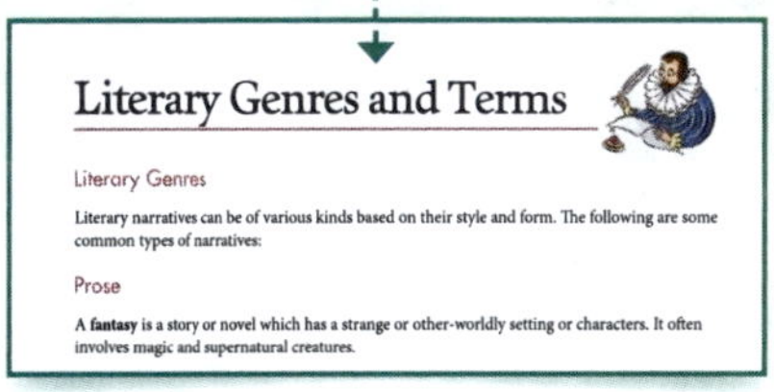

Literary Genres and Terms

Literary Genres

Literary narratives can be of various kinds based on their style and form. The following are some common types of narratives:

Prose

A **fantasy** is a story or novel which has a strange or other-worldly setting or characters. It often involves magic and supernatural creatures.

Read More

- Contains extra suggested reading for the avid learner to foster love for literature

Assessments

- Includes a Test Paper in Workbooks 3-8 based on the principle of SAFAL that encourages competency-based learning

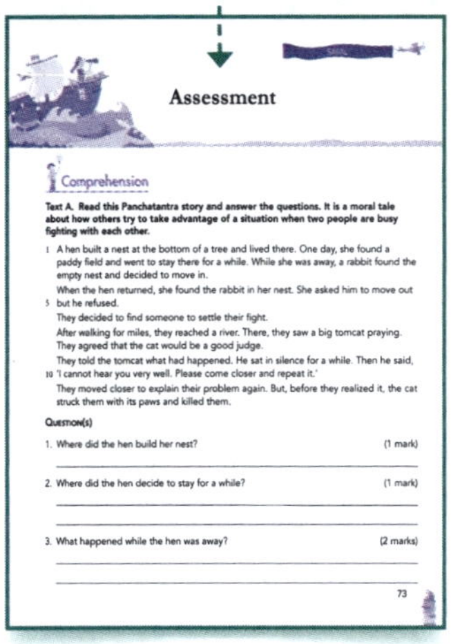

Assessment

Comprehension

Text A. Read this Panchatantra story and answer the questions. It is a moral tale about how others try to take advantage of a situation when two people are busy fighting with each other.

A hen built a nest at the bottom of a tree and lived there. One day, she found a paddy field and went to stay there for a while. While she was away, a rabbit found the empty nest and decided to move in.
When the hen returned, she found the rabbit in her nest. She asked him to move out but he refused.
They decided to find someone to settle their fight.
After walking for miles, they reached a river. There, they saw a big tomcat praying. They agreed that the cat would be a good judge.
They told the tomcat what had happened. He sat in silence for a while. Then he said, 'I cannot hear you very well. Please come closer and repeat it.'
They moved closer to explain their problem again. But, before they realized it, the cat struck them with its paws and killed them.

Question(s)

1. Where did the hen build her nest? (1 mark)
2. Where did the hen decide to stay for a while? (1 mark)
3. What happened while the hen was away? (2 marks)

73

Poster

- Literature and vocabulary games, and activities based on distinct themes

Icons

Revised Engaging English aims to equip students with various skills outlined in the National Education Policy, 2020, that target the holistic education of the learner. Take a look at the various icons used to showcase these skills.

Twenty-first Century Skills

Mastering these skills will equip learners to face the challenges of a rapidly changing, digital society.

Happiness Content

The idea underlying 'Happiness Content', a part of the 'Happiness Curriculum', is that learning should be an enjoyable process. For knowledge to bring joy, learning must focus on concept-based rather than rote learning.

1 HC **Learning and Awareness**

Exploring happiness through Learning and Awareness

2 HC **Feelings**

Experiencing happiness in relationships through Feelings

3 HC **Active Participation**

Happiness through Active Participation

SUSTAINABLE DEVELOPMENT GOALS

The Sustainable Development Goals (SDGs) were adopted by the United Nations in 2015 as a universal call to action to end poverty, protect the planet, and ensure that by 2030, all people enjoy peace and prosperity. The 17 SDGs recognize that development must balance social, economic and environmental sustainability.

Art Integration

The arts, or the fine arts, are painting, sculpture, architecture, poetry, music, literature and dance. Art-integrated experiential learning uses concepts from the arts to provide learners a multi-disciplinary experience.

Cross-curricular Content

The cross-curricular approach to teaching recognises that subjects are inter-linked, and for effective concept-acquisition, they must be taught in synergy with each other.

Math

Science

History

Geography

Acknowledgements

The publishers wish to thank and acknowledge the following for granting us permission to use copyright material:

Ruskin Bond for *A New Flower*. Reprinted with the permission of the author; Aaron Shepard for *The Four Puppets*. Reprinted with the permission of the author; Romila Thapar for *The Barber's Wife*. Copyright © Romila Thapar 1991. Reprinted with the permission of the author; *Tintin in Tibet*, written and illustrated by Hergé. Reprinted by permission of Moulinsart SA. Copyright © 1958, Hergé; Arden Davidson for *Be Careful What You Wish For*. Reprinted with the permission of the author; Harold Alfred Manhood for *Shall We Ghost*. Reprinted with the permission of Sundial Press UK.

The publishers have applied for permission for the following:
The Secret Cavern by Margaret Widdemer, *Sick* by Shel Silverstein, *An Old Friend* by Jayanti Adhikari, *Pepper the Phantom Pet* by Paro Anand.
Acknowledgements for these texts will be made in the future editions of the book.

Every effort has been made to trace copyright holders and to obtain their permission for the use of copyright material. However, in some instances, we have been unable to trace the owners of the copyright pieces published here. The authors and publishers will gladly receive any information enabling them to rectify any error or omission in subsequent editions.

Illustrations

Inside: Page 6: SDG logo and icons: https://www.un.org/sustainabledevelopment/
The content of this publication has not been approved by the United Nations and does not reflect the views of the United Nations or its officials or Member States. **Page 11:** InfiniteGraphic, stockillustration, Svitlana Varfolomieieva, graphic-bee, seamartini; **13:** dedMazay, Easy_Company; **14:** Benjavisa, weniworks, lukbar, Ja_inter, bortonia; **15:** lankogal, zaricm; **16:** johnnylemonseed, duescreatius1; **17:** mi_007; **18:** colematt, sabelskaya, apzats; **19:** Anwar Hussain; **22:** dedMazay; **23:** Benjavisa; **25:** Anwar Hussain; **27:** sabelskaya; **32:** dedMazay; **33:** Benjavisa; **37:** sabelskaya; **39:** tachyglossus, dedMazay; **40:** Benjavisa; **41:** nopember30; **45:** sabelskaya; **46:** Good_Stock; **47:** tachyglossus; **50:** Benjavisa; **53:** sabelskaya; **54:** scibak, Nerthuz, 3DSculptor, oatawa, aapsky; **56:** bonezboyz, JPL-Caltech/NASA; **57:** Luca_ingi; **60:** johnnylemonseed; **61:** larryrains; **62:** Natalia Saudi, Vyacheslav Motserenkov; **63:** sabelskaya; **64:** stevegraham; **65:** Hana Kruzikova; **66:** klyaksun; dedMazay; **69:** Irina Cheremisinova, yulianas; **70:** engabito; **71:** sabelskaya; **72:** NicholasKinney; **76:** dedMazay; **77:** Benjavisa, kbeis; **80:** sabelskaya; **81:** dutourdumonde, DanielPrudek; **86:** Natalie_; **87:** dedMazay, PictureLake; **89:** Victor_Brave; **90:** cenkerdem, istock; **91:** Easy_Company; **92:** sabelskaya; **93:** Big_Ryan; **94:** tachyglossus; **99:** arryrains, sabelskaya; **100:** Aleutie; **103:** dedMazay; **109:** IrynaDanyliuk; **111:** peanutpie; **116:** TopVectors, Natalie; **120:** rosadu, **125:** StarLineArts; **129:** dedMazay; **133:** sabelskaya; **134:** inktycoon, zaricm, Val_Iva, Vect0r0vich, ssnjaytuturkhi; **135:** dedMazay; **144:** tachyglossus; **150:** ilyaliren; **161:** Getty.

Detailed Contents

Unit	Theme	Comprehension	Way with Words	Grammar in Use	Study Skills	Listening and Speaking	Pen It Down
1. The Arrow and the Song	Music and the Arts	• Questions • Reference to context	• Homonyms, homographs and homophones	• Subject and predicate	• Spell Check: spelling of words ending with *-al* and *-el*	• Listening to directions and tracing a route on a map	• Process writing: Creating a song
2. A New Flower	Nature	• Questions • Reference to context	• Compound words • Proverbs	• Articles • Nouns: Gender	• Pronounce Well: different pronunciation of the words containing *-ough*	• Listening to a description and giving a description	• Essay writing
3. The Four Puppets	Southeast Asia	• Questions • Reference to context	• Phrasal verbs	• Adjectives: quality, quantity, number, demonstrative, possessive and interrogative • Prepositions: time, place and movement • *For* and *since*	• Pronounce Well: syllables and syllabification	• Pair work: framing questions for answers	• Writing a short composition
4. The Fisherman	Seafaring	• Questions • Reference to context	• Prefixes *un-* and *mis-* • Collocations	• Subject-verb agreement • Subject and object pronouns	• Use Your Dictionary: abbreviations	• Practising tongue twisters • Role-play: making offers	• Writing a composition about a profession
5. The Birth of the Seasons	Mythological Tales	• Questions • Reference to context	• Antonyms	• Types of sentences and their transformation • Abstract nouns	• Spell Check: missing letters	• Listening to words and classifying them	• Rewriting the story in the first person
6. Roving on the Red Planet	Space Exploration	• Questions • Reference to context	• Crossword • Words related to space • Measures of uncountable nouns	• Present and past continuous tenses • Forming *Wh-* questions	• Spell Check: words ending with *-ar* and *-er*	• Role playing an imaginary conversation	• Writing an autobiographical account of an inanimate object • Writing a notice
Be Creative!							
7. The Secret Cavern	Imagination	• Questions • Reference to context	• Suffix *-ly*	• Apostrophe for plural possessives • Apostrophe in contractions • Interjections	• Spell Check: making new words by adding *-ing*	• Practise saying consonant blends like *sk*, *bl*, *mp*, *ch* • Narrating incidents in groups	• Writing a descriptive composition with an illustration
8. The Barber's Wife	Community and Neighbourhood	• Questions • Reference to context	• Commonly confused words	• Demonstrative and interrogative pronouns • Comparison of adjectives	• Spell Check: commonly misspelt words	• Listening to instructions and sequencing • Story-telling • Listening to sounds and identifying emotions	• Sequencing and writing a picture composition

Unit	Theme	Comprehension	Way with Words	Grammar in Use	Study Skills	Listening and Speaking	Pen It Down
9. Tintin in Tibet	India's Neighbours	• Questions • Reference to context	• Prefix *-un* • Phrasal verbs with *run*	• Conditional Sentences with *if* • Coordinating conjunctions	• Pronounce Well: words with silent letters	• Role-play: making an apology	• Writing an informal letter
10. Sick	Healthy Living	• Questions • Reference to context	• Different types of doctors • Similes	• Determiners: *many, much, most, some, any* • Future continuous tense • Irregular verbs	• Pronounce Well: pronunciation of *i* in various words	• Listening to a poem and marking true or false	• Writing a few sentences describing a health condition
11. The Incident of the Letter	Suspense and Mystery	• Questions • Reference to context	• Analogies	• Present and past perfect tense	• Pronounce Well: words with the letter *s*	• Listening to a story and answering questions	• Writing a formal letter • Writing a message accepting or declining an invitation
12. Be Careful What You Wish For	Ambition	• Questions • Multiple Choice Questions	• Word meanings • Making sentences	• Direct and indirect speech	• Use Your Dictionary: phrasal verbs with *off*	• Reading and identifying alliteration	• Writing a poem
Be Creative!							
13. An Old Friend	Friends and Family	• Questions • Reference to context	• Polite requests in the form of questions	• Inappropriate shift in verb tense • Comparison of adverbs	• Pronounce Well: words with the letter *u*	• Listening, researching and speaking on a given topic	• Writing a diary entry
14. Shall We Ghost	Spooks and the Supernatural	• Questions • Reference to context	• Naming the various spaces in a house • Making sentences	• Modals • Punctuation	• Spell Check: identifying correct spellings	• Listening to and identifying expressions of agreement or disagreement	• Writing a story
15. Rain in the Hills	Nature	• Questions • Reference to context	• Sense words	• Prepositions: usage of *in* and *into*	• Use Your Dictionary: finding words related to train travel	• Listening to and identifying short and long vowel sounds	• Writing a newspaper report
16. Pepper, the Phantom Pet — I	Humorous Tales	• Questions • Reference to context	• Idioms • Making sentences	• Question tags • Adverbs: place, manner, degree and time	• Pronounce Well: words with the letter *q*	• Listening to and answering funny questions	• Writing an e-mail
17. Pepper, the Phantom Pet — II	Community and Neighbourhood	• Questions • Reference to context	• Fields of study • Idioms	• Active and passive voice	• Spell Check: words with endings *-ible* and *-able*	• Debate on a given topic	• Writing a dialogue
Be Creative!							
Literary Genres and Terms							

Contents

1

The Arrow and the Song

lyric poem

Henry Wadsworth Longfellow

Let's Get Started

ART INTEGRATION

Look at the following images of Indian musical instruments. Complete their names using the picture clues and descriptions.

V _ _ _ _
(a stringed instrument used in Indian classical music)

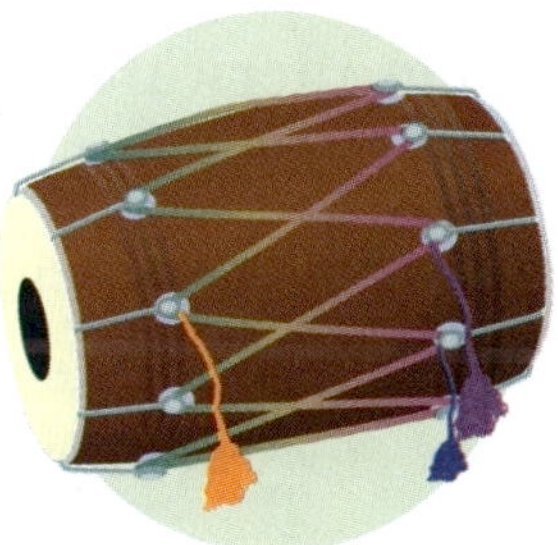

D _ _ _ _ _
(a two-headed hand drum, used as a percussion instrument in Indian music)

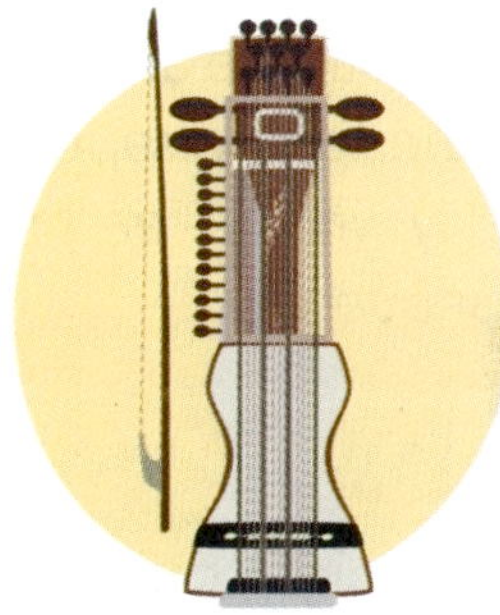

S _ _ _ _ _ _
(a bowed, stringed instrument, played in Indian traditional and folk music)

_ _ _ L _ _
(a stringed instrument played with a bow and used in classical music)

S _ _ _ _
(a stringed instrument, used mainly in Hindustani music)

S _ _ _ _
(a stringed instrument from the Indian classical tradition)

HC **Feelings:** Contributions in relationships (friends)

Reading

Read this poem about the power of music and the value of friendship.

Literary terms

1. This is an example of a **metaphor**. Here, the song is being compared to human breath which once released, can never be taken in again.

2. This is an example of **repetition**, which is used for emphasis. Here, both the arrow and the song disappear quickly with far-reaching consequences.

I shot an arrow into the air,
It fell to earth, I knew not where;
For, so **swiftly** it flew, the **sight**
Could not follow it in its flight.

I breathed[1] a song into the air,
It fell to earth, I knew not where[2];
For who has sight so **keen** and strong,
That it can follow the flight of song?

Long, long **afterward**, in an **oak**
I found the arrow, still unbroke;
And the song, from beginning to end,
I found again in the heart of a friend.

What did the speaker breathe into the air?

swiftly: rapidly, quickly
sight: (here) eyes
keen: sharp
afterward: American English for *afterwards*
oak: a type of tree

Wordwise

The word **shot** can be used in different ways:

- *shot an arrow:* the act of shooting
- *a shot of espresso:* a small measure of black coffee
- *give it a shot:* attempt or try
- *get a shot:* get an injection

About the poet

Henry Wadsworth Longfellow (1807–1882) was an American poet and professor at Harvard College. He was known for his lyric poems and was the most famous poet of his times. His books include *Voices of the Night* and *Ballads and Other Poems.*

Comprehension

Quick Recap

A. Answer these questions.

1. What are the things that the poet sent into the air?
2. Where did the song fall?
3. Why could the sight not follow the song?
4. What are the arrow and the song used as metaphors for, in the poem?

B. Read the lines from the poem and answer the questions.

1. *For, so swiftly it flew, the sight*
   Could not follow it in its flight.
   a. What does 'it' refer to?
   b. Where did 'it' fall?
   c. Where did the speaker find 'it' later?
2. *I found it again in the heart of a friend.*
   a. Who is the speaker here?
   b. What does he find in the heart of his friend?
   c. Why does he say that he found 'it' from 'beginning to end'?

Life Skills and Values

friendship, kindness

Think and answer.

1. What, according to you, is the message of this poem?
2. Write about an incident in your life in which you experienced the negative impact of words.

Way with Words

Homonyms

Look at these sentences.

Could not follow it in its **flight**.

I could not catch the **flight** as I was late.

The word **flight** has been used in two different ways in the sentences.

Words that have the same spelling but have different meanings are known as **homonyms**.

A. Complete the sentences using the correct homonyms from the box.

cold   right   play   watch

1. a. The ____________ based on Shakespeare's *Hamlet* was very well presented.
   b. They have gone to ____________ in the park.
2. a. Please ____________ your step.
   b. Where have you kept my ____________?
3. a. He took the ____________ decision.
   b. Take a ____________ turn from the crossing and you will reach the mall.
4. a. It is too ____________ outside.
   b. He is down with a ____________ and a cough.

Homographs

Read these sentences.

I shot an arrow with a **bow**.

Please **bow** after your speech.

The word **bow** has different meanings and pronunciations in both sentences.

In the first sentence, the word **bow** means 'the curved instrument with which an arrow is shot', while in the second sentence, it means 'bending from one's waist in front of people, out of respect'.

Words that have the same spelling but have different meanings and pronunciations, are called **homographs**.

B. Two meanings of the homographs are given in the box. Pick the correct one and write it down next to the meanings.

row	close	tear	lead	minute	live

1. water from one's eyes; to rip things like paper __________
2. time equal to 60 seconds; tiny __________
3. a fight; push a boat forward on water with an oar __________
4. survive; something that is happening at the moment __________
5. a natural element; guide someone __________
6. nearby; the opposite of 'open' __________

C. Now make sentences with each of the words in the previous exercise to show the difference in their meanings.

Homophones

Homophones are words that sound alike but have different meanings and spellings.

Example: It fell to earth, I **knew** not where;
I bought **new** shoes for my friend.

The words **knew** and **new** are homophones.

D. Choose the correct homophones to complete the sentences.

1. Our new __________ is very strict. (principal/principle)
2. Wearing a helmet __________ the risk of a head injury. (lessons/lessens)
3. I need to get the __________ of my cycle repaired. (pedal/peddle)
4. Dust the __________ on the board before rolling the dough. (flour/flower)

Grammar in Use

Subject and Predicate

We know that a sentence is a group of words which makes complete sense. Every complete sentence has a **subject** and a **predicate**.

The **subject** of the sentence is *what* or *whom* the sentence is about. The **predicate** tells us something about the subject.

Example: I shot an arrow. (**I**: subject; **shot an arrow**: predicate)

The subject of a sentence might be either a noun or a pronoun. The predicate of the sentence contains the verb. A sentence may have only one subject or two or more subjects, joined by conjunctions like **and**.

The subject is followed by the verb in most sentences. Sometimes, the order is changed and the verb comes before the subject, depending on the type of sentence.

Examples: Where is the bag? (interrogative)
Never have I felt so embarrassed! (exclamatory)
(You) Pass the sugar. (imperative)

A. Circle the subject and underline the predicate in each of these sentences.

1. (You) Get me a glass of water.
2. Rohit and Ramita saw a beautiful red bird on the tree.
3. Waiting by the gate was my friend.
4. My favourite month is March.
5. How lovely the roses are!
6. Is the cake box in the cupboard?
7. There is a rat in the attic.

B. Read the following phrases and identify them as subject or predicate.

1. read her book
2. failed her math test
3. My friends
4. wagged his tail
5. His favourite show
6. the cricket match
7. The family
8. smiled and waved
9. stung my arm

Study Skills

Spell Check

Look at the spelling of these words carefully.

digital	eventual	abdominal	casual	financial
parallel	colonel	funnel	label	shovel

A. Complete these words with -al or -el.

1. nas __ __
2. kenn __ __
3. chann __ __
4. vir __ __
5. marv __ __
6. liber __ __
7. tow __ __
8. hospit __ __
9. trib __ __

B. Read the clues and guess the words. All the words end in -al or -el.

1. accompanied by music ________
2. form of word used to denote more than one ________
3. a wrapped gift sent by post ________
4. a place where travellers stay ________

Listening and Speaking

Listen carefully to the instructions given of the path taken by the arrow after it was shot. After listening, trace the route of the arrow on the map.

The arrow left the bow and flew straight till it hit a tower. From there, it turned right and travelled four paces till it reached a crossroads. From that point, it turned right and went past the monument. Finally, it was stuck in an oak tree's trunk, which was in Citizen Park.

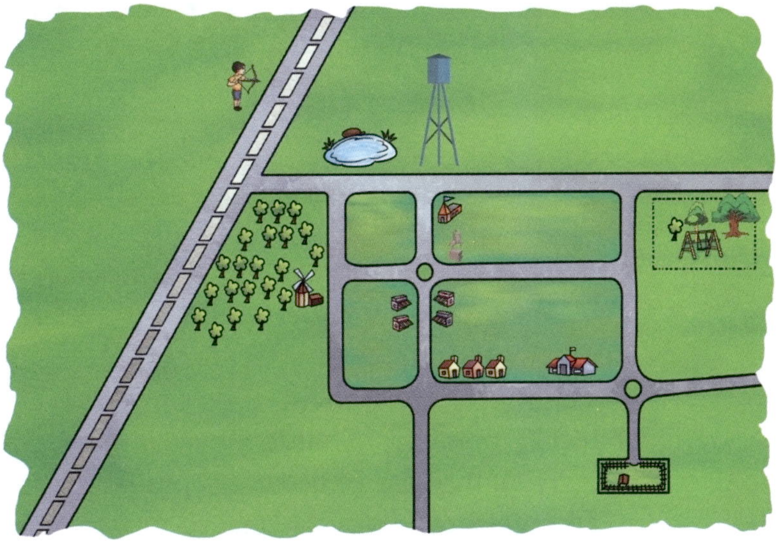

Pen it Down

Process writing helps to focus on the different stages and aspects of writing, in a systematic manner. These stages are: selecting the topic, understanding the target readers, planning, drafting, revising, editing and completing the final draft.

Write down the process for creating a song in five steps. Then, follow the process you have outlined to create a simple song of your own in six lines.

Consider the following aspects while writing the steps:
- topic or central idea of your song
- rhyming words you can use
- melody and a suitable title for the song

Self Assessment

Now I can

- read and enjoy a poem about friendship.
- use homonyms, homophones and homographs.
- identify the subject and the predicate in a sentence.
- follow a route on a map using landmarks and understand process writing.

2

Nature

A New Flower

Ruskin Bond

SUSTAINABLE DEVELOPMENT GOALS

15 LIFE ON LAND

Let's Get Started

The United Nations Sustainable Development Goal 15 highlights the need to manage forests and halt the loss of flora and fauna. Certain insects and animals help flowers bloom, and we should do our best to protect them.

In this word grid, identify the names of some flowers as well as animals and insects that help flowers bloom and grow.

F	L	Y	J	I	W	H	O	N	E	Y	B	E	E	S	M
M	K	A	E	N	B	E	T	M	O	D	F	L	U	A	A
G	H	A	O	E	I	A	O	A	P	F	F	N	B	D	R
B	P	L	W	O	B	U	T	T	E	R	F	L	Y	Y	I
P	R	U	A	N	D	O	S	G	W	Y	G	N	K	M	G
O	C	S	E	K	A	J	P	W	L	R	T	Q	U	E	O
P	J	R	O	S	E	T	A	B	G	H	A	E	L	Z	L
P	N	Q	A	I	N	R	F	M	O	T	H	R	O	Y	D
Y	I	M	N	D	R	O	N	F	G	H	I	T	T	U	F
B	G	W	M	G	H	B	D	E	P	S	N	K	U	L	U
O	S	U	N	F	L	O	W	E	R	N	M	E	S	Z	S
R	N	L	G	H	N	W	A	S	P	O	T	E	E	A	W
A	H	B	A	T	A	C	J	E	B	E	E	T	L	E	E
J	A	S	M	I	N	E	U	C	L	A	K	E	E	I	I

Common Indian flowers and their pollinators

marigold	lotus	rose	sunflower	poppy	jasmine
butterfly	moth	honeybee	wasp	beetle	fly

HC **Learning and Awareness:** Humans and other orders

Reading

Do you like flowers? Usha, a young girl, sees a beautiful yellow flower on the hillside. That night, the delicate flower is washed away by heavy rains. Will Usha see the flower again? Read the story to find out.

It was the first day of spring (according to the Hindu calendar), but here in the Himalayas it still seemed mid-winter. A cold wind hummed and whistled through the pines, while dark rain clouds were swept along by the west wind only to be **thrust** back by the east wind.

I was climbing the **steep** road to my cottage at the top of the hill when I was overtaken by nine-year-old Usha hurrying back from school. She had tied a scarf round her head to keep her hair from blowing. Her dark hair, black eyes and pink cheeks could be seen all the more clearly because of the patches of snow still lying on the hillside. 'Look,' she said, pointing, 'A new flower!'

It was a single, butter-yellow blossom and it stood out like a bright star against the **drab** winter grass. I hadn't seen anything like it before and had no idea what its name might be. No doubt its existence was recorded in some **botanical tome**. But for me, it was a new discovery.

'Shall I pick it for you?' asked Usha.

'No, don't,' I said. 'It may be the only one. If we pluck it, there may not be any more. Let's leave it there and see if it seeds.'

We **scrambled** up the slope and examined the flower more closely. It was very delicate and soft-petalled, looking as if it might fall at any moment. 'It will be finished if it rains,' said Usha.

And it did rain that night—rain mingled with **sleet** and hail. It rattled and **swished** on the **corrugated** tin roof; but in the morning, the sun came out.

Did You Know? G.K.

The Hindu calendar is based on the position of the sun and the moon while the western calendar is based only on the position of the sun.

thrust: pushed suddenly or violently

steep: (here) having a slope

drab: not bright

botanical: relating to plants

tome: a large, heavy, scholarly book

scrambled: (here) climbed up using their hands to help them

sleet: rain containing some ice

swished: moved with a hissing sound

corrugated: grooved

Literary term

1. This is a **metaphor**. Here, the writer compares the newly opened flower buds to two small stars.

thickets: dense groups of bushes or trees

retreated: moved away when faced with opposition

baleful: threatening to hurt somebody

nasturtiums: plants with round leaves and orange, yellow or red flowers

discretion: the quality of being careful

valour: bravery

sizing up: understanding

unfurled: spread or opened something, normally a flag or an umbrella

dignity: honour, pride

freelance: working independently and not in any company on a regular salary

I walked up the road without really expecting to see the flower again. And Usha had been right. The flower had disappeared in the storm. But two other buds, unnoticed by us the day before, had opened. It was as though two tiny stars had fallen to Earth in the night[1].

I did not see Usha that day; but the following day when we met on the road, I showed her the fresh blossoms. And they were still there, two days later, when I passed by; but so were two goats, grazing on the short grass and thorny **thickets** of the slope. I had no idea if they were partial to these particular flowers, but I did know that goats would eat almost anything and I was taking no chances. Scrambling up the steep slope, I began to shoo them away. One goat **retreated**, but the other lowered its horns, gave me a **baleful** look and refused to move.

It reminded me a little of my grandfather's pet goat who had once pushed a visiting official into a bed of **nasturtiums**; so I allowed **discretion** to be the better part of **valour** and backed away. Just then Usha came along and, **sizing up** the situation, came to the rescue. She **unfurled** her pretty blue umbrella and advanced on the goat shouting at it in goat-language. (She had her own goats at home.) The beast retreated and the flowers (and my **dignity**) were saved.

As the days grew warmer, the flowers faded and finally disappeared. I forgot all about them and so did Usha. There were lessons and exams for her to worry about, and rent and electricity bills to occupy a **freelance** writer's thoughts. The months passed; summer and autumn came and went, with their own more showy blooms; and in no time at all, winter returned with cold winds blowing from all directions.

One day I heard Usha calling to me from the hillside. I looked up and saw her standing behind a little cluster of golden, star-shaped flowers—not, perhaps, as **spectacular** as Wordsworth's field of golden daffodils, but nevertheless, an **enchanting** sight for one who had played a small part in making sure they lived.

Where there had been one flowering plant, there were now several. Usha and I **speculated** on the prospect of the entire hillside being covered with the flowers in a few years' time.

I still do not know the botanical name for the little flower. I cannot remember long Latin names, anyway, but Usha tells me that she has seen it growing near her father's village on the next mountain and that the hill people call it *Basant*, which means spring.

Although I am just a little disappointed that we are not, after all, the discoverers of a new species, this is **outweighed** by pure pleasure in knowing that the flower **flourishes** in **adversity.** May it multiply!

spectacular: eye-catching
enchanting: delightful
speculated: guessed
outweighed: overcome
flourishes: grows well
adversity: difficult situation

Did You Know? Science

All plants have a common name and a botanical name. The botanical names are in Latin and have two parts, which carry information about the plant.

About the author

Ruskin Bond (1934–) is one of the most loved Indian authors of children's literature in English. Nature is often a theme in his stories. He wrote his first novel, *The Room on the Roof*, when he was seventeen. He was awarded the Padma Shri in 1999 for his contribution to children's literature. He lives in Mussourie, a hill station in Uttarakhand.

Comprehension

Quick Recap

A. Answer these questions in a few lines.

1. Describe the weather in the Himalayas on the first day of spring.
2. Where was Usha coming from and what had she done to keep her hair from blowing?
3. What did the flower that Usha showed to the narrator look like?
4. What are the various seasons described in the story? Write some of the words that are used to describe the seasons.

5. What did the narrator find when he went to see the flower the day after it had rained?
6. How did Usha drive the goats away?

B. Read the lines from the story and answer the questions.

1. *'Shall I pick it for you?'*
   a. Who said these words and to whom?
   b. What does the word 'it' refer to?
   c. What reply did the listener give?
2. *May it multiply!*
   a. What does 'it' refer to?
   b. What does 'multiply' mean here?
   c. What were the adversities despite which 'it' flourished?

Life Skills and Values

appreciating nature

Think and answer.

1. What kind of a person, do you think, is the narrator? Write a character sketch in about five sentences.
2. What do you think the phrase 'my dignity was saved' means? Why does the narrator think his dignity was saved by Usha?
3. Why did Usha and the narrator forget about the flowers as the days became warmer?

21ST CENTURY Critical Thinking

Way with Words

Compound Words

In this story, we came across words like **star-shaped**, **soft-petalled** and **mid-winter**. These are examples of **compound words**.

A. Join the words in the box to make compound words. Then, make sentences with each compound word.

tooth	noon	white	chair	mid	board
arm	black	paste	after	washed	night

Proverbs

'Discretion is the better part of valour' is an example of a proverb. It means, it is often wise to stop oneself from doing or saying something which may seem bold and brave but may end up causing trouble for oneself.

A **proverb** is a well-known phrase or sentence that gives advice or says something that is generally true.

Examples: Honesty is the best policy.
Birds of a feather flock together.
The early bird catches the worm.

B. Match the columns to complete the proverbs. Then, find out what they mean.

A	B
1. A bird in hand	a. is the best sauce.
2. A friend in need	b. is not gold.
3. Actions speak	c. seldom bite.
4. All that glitters	d. is worth two in the bush.
5. An apple a day	e. than never.
6. Barking dogs	f. louder than words.
7. Better late	g. is a friend indeed.
8. Hunger	h. keeps the doctor away.

Grammar in Use

Articles

The indefinite articles – *a* and *an* – are used to refer to any singular noun.

Indefinite articles indicate that a noun refers to a general idea rather than a particular thing.

The article **a** is used with words beginning with consonant sounds and **an** is used with words beginning with vowel sounds.

Examples: **A** cold wind hummed and whistled through the pines.
She unfurled **an** umbrella.

The **definite article** – *the* – is used to refer to a particular noun, and can be used with both singular and plural, and uncountable nouns.

Example: **The** flower had disappeared in **the** storm.

Sometimes, articles are omitted altogether before certain uncountable nouns, such as **air**, **water**, **sugar** and **happiness**. We do not use **a** and **an** with these uncountable nouns.

Examples: There is no **sugar** in the tea.
Happiness is a state of mind.

A. Fill the blanks with a/an where required.

Dorothy lived in the great Kansas prairies, with Uncle Henry, who was _____ farmer, and _____ Aunt Em, who was _____ excellent farmer's wife. Their house was _____ ancient-looking cottage. There were _____ four walls, _____ floor and _____ roof, which made one room; and this room contained _____ rusty looking cooking stove, _____ old cupboard for the dishes, _____ table, three or four chairs, and the beds. Uncle Henry and Aunt Em had _____ big bed in one corner, and Dorothy had _____ little bed in another corner. There was no attic at all, and no cellar, except _____ small hole, dug in the ground, called a cyclone cellar, where the family could go in case one of those great whirlwinds arose, mighty enough to crush any building in its path. It was reached by _____ trap-door in the middle of the floor, from which _____ ladder led down into _____ small, dark hole.

B. Tick [✓] the correct articles in these sentences.

1. What **a/an/the** beautiful sight it was!
2. That was quite **a/an/the** interesting story.
3. Steps are being taken to clean up **a/an/the** Ganges.
4. **The/A/An** basket full of apples is kept on **a/an/the** table.
5. **The/An/A** train leaves at 7 o'clock in the morning.
6. She missed her school bus as she reached **a/an/the** bus stop very late.

Nouns: Gender

You have learned that nouns can be classified into four genders: masculine, feminine, common and neuter. **Examples:** king, princess, cousin, rose

C. Identify the gender of the nouns in bold in these sentences.

1. The **doctor** was examining the **patient**.
2. The **reporter** was covering the event live with a **cameraman**.
3. The **drake** was grooming its **feathers**.
4. The **mare** and the **rooster** were **friends**.

5. The **seamstress** made a lovely wedding gown for the **bride**.
6. The **farmer** harvested the crops with the help of other **villagers**.
7. The **peacock** has a long beautiful tail while the **peahen** doesn't.
8. The **teacher** was given an award by the **minister**.

Study Skills

Pronounce Well

The words **through**, **though** and **thought** are all pronounced differently. The letter combination *-ough* has many pronunciations depending on its position in a word.

Put the following words in the correct column, so that they rhyme with the given words.

plough	tough	trough	thought	through	nought
thorough	brought	sought	enough	dough	cough

rough	bough	bought	odd ones

Listening and Speaking

Listen to the description of a rose. Then, form pairs and describe a flower of your choice. Each pair will speak for two minutes.

Your description can include the following points:
- its name in English and in your mother tongue
- where you saw it: park, home, forest, botanical garden, florist
- a description of its colour, shape, size and overall appearance
- if possible, its Latin name (you will have to look this up on the Internet or ask your science teacher)
- why you chose this flower over others

HC Observing natural entities

Pen it Down

Creativity

Write an essay about a hill station you visited. Describe how you spent your time there and the differences you noticed between a hill station and the plains.

You can include the following points:
- the name of the hill station and where it is located
- when you went there and a description of the place
- what activities you participated in
- what local food you ate there and the things you bought
- what you liked about the place and why

Self Assessment

Now I can

- read a story about how a simple flower creates a bond between a man and a little girl.
- use compound words, some common proverbs, articles and gender in nouns.
- pronounce *-ough-* words and describe a flower.
- write an essay about a trip to a hill station.

Read More

The Blue Umbrella: This story by Ruskin Bond is about a little girl, Binya, and her fascination with a blue umbrella. The beautiful blue umbrella makes her the envy of the entire village.

The Why-Why Girl: This story by Mahasweta Devi is about Moina, a very curious tribal girl. She is so full of questions that the postmaster calls her the 'why-why girl'.

folktale

3

Southeast Asia

The Four Puppets

Aaron Shepard

Let's Get Started

Read the sentences about the country of Myanmar and fill in the blanks with the correct option.

1. Myanmar, or Burma, as it was earlier known, is a country in Southeast ______ (India/Asia).
2. Myanmar shares its ______ (walls/borders) with India, Bangladesh, China, Thailand and Laos.
3. In ______ (ancient/recent) times, Myanmar was a centre of Buddhist culture. Even today, most ______ (Burmese/Bhutanese) are followers of the Buddha.
4. Myanmar was a part of the British ______ (Empire/ capital) until its independence in 1948. Many Indians lived and worked in the region at that time.
5. For much of its independence, Myanmar has been under military ______ (ruling/rule). From 2015 to 2020, the country enjoyed democracy. In 2021, the military took control of the country again.

Women and children in 19th century Myanmar

HC **Learning and Awareness:** Humans and other orders

Reading

Have you ever seen a puppet? Read this Burmese folktale about a young man who seeks his fortune and gets differing advice from four talking puppets. Find out what happens

honourable: deserving to be respected

virtue: a good quality

ogre: a man-eating giant

mystic: having spiritual powers or qualities that are difficult to understand or explain

sorcerer: a person who performs magic by using the power of spirits

hermit: a person who lives alone, away from people and society

when he follows the advice of these puppets.

Once there was a puppet maker who had a son named Aung. The father always hoped his son would grow up to be a puppet maker too. But to Aung, such a life was far from exciting.

'Father,' said Aung one day, 'I've decided to leave home and seek my fortune.'

The puppet maker looked up sadly from his work. 'The life of a puppet maker is an **honourable** one. But if you must go, let me give you companions for your journey.'

He showed his son four wooden puppets he had made. 'Each,' he said, 'has its own **virtue** and value.'

The first puppet was the king of the gods. The puppet maker said, 'His virtue is wisdom.'

The second puppet was a green-faced **ogre.** 'His virtue is strength.'

The third was a **mystic sorcerer.** 'His virtue is knowledge.'

The fourth was a holy **hermit.** 'His virtue is goodness.'

He told his son, 'Each of these virtues can help you on your way. But remember, strength and knowledge must always serve wisdom and goodness.'

Aung started off the next day. On his shoulder he carried a bamboo pole, with food and clothing tied at one end, and the puppets hanging by their strings from the other.

When night came, Aung found himself deep in the jungle. He stopped beneath a banyan tree.

'This looks like a good place to sleep,' he said to himself. 'But I wonder if it's safe.'

Then, Aung had an idea. 'I think I'll ask one of the puppets!' He turned with a smile to the king of the gods. 'Tell me, is it safe here?'

To his amazement, the puppet came alive. It got down from the pole and grew life size.

'Aung,' said the god, 'look around you. That is the first step to wisdom. If you fail to see what is right before you, how easy it will be for others to misguide you!' Then, the puppet hung again from the pole.

When Aung got over his shock, he looked carefully all around the tree. There, in the soft earth, were the tracks of a tiger! That night he slept not on the ground but in the branches above. He was glad he did, for in the middle of the night he saw a tiger come **prowling** below him.

The next day took Aung into the mountains, where he saw a caravan coming along the road below. A dozen bullock carts were piled high with costly goods.

'That caravan must belong to a rich merchant,' Aung told himself.

He turned to the ogre. 'Tell me, how can I gain such riches?'

prowling: moving about restlessly in search of prey

landslide: a large amount of earth and rocks falling down a cliff or the side of a mountain

gaping: (here) staring in amazement, with mouth wide open

huddled: holding arms and legs close to the body

'If you have strength, you can take whatever you like,' boomed the ogre. He stamped his foot and the earth shook.

Below them, dirt and rocks broke loose in a **landslide** and blocked the road. The terrified drivers jumped from their carts and ran off.

Aung hurried down and rushed from one cart to another, **gaping** at the rich fabrics and precious metals. 'All of it is mine!' he cried.

Just then, Aung heard a sob. **Huddled** in one of the carts was a lovely young woman his own age.

'I won't hurt you,' said Aung gently. 'Who are you?'

'My name is Mala,' she said in a small voice. 'My father is the owner of this caravan. We were on our way to meet him.'

Aung fell in love with her. He wanted to keep Mala with him forever. 'Don't worry,' he said. 'I'll take you with me and care for you.'

Mala sat up angrily. 'Take me, like you're taking everything else! But you're just a thief and I'll never, ever speak to you!'

Aung was shocked. Was he really just a thief?

The ogre came up beside him. 'Don't listen to her. The important thing is you got what you wanted. Now, let's go.'

That afternoon, they came out of the mountains, not far from the capital city. Aung turned to the sorcerer, 'What should I do with these riches?'

The puppet came to life, as Mala looked on with wide eyes. 'If you want your wealth to grow,' he said, 'you must learn the secrets of nature.'

He tapped Aung with his wand and together they rose high in the air. Looking down, Aung saw everything. He could tell what land was best for farming and which mountains held gold and silver.

'This is wonderful!' said Aung. 'I can help everyone with what I know!'

'Knowledge is power. Why not keep it for yourself instead? Isn't that what other people do?' asked the sorcerer.

'I suppose so,' said Aung.

So they came to the capital city. Aung became a merchant, and with the help of the ogre and the sorcerer, he grew many times richer. He bought a palace and kept the puppets in a special room.

Did You Know? History

Puppetry is an art form believed to be about 30,000 years old. People use puppets to communicate their ideas. India has a very ancient tradition of puppetry, with mentions in the *Mahabharata* too.

headdress: a covering worn on the head on special occasions

But Aung was not happy, for Mala still would not speak to him. One day, he placed before her a **headdress** set with large rubies, sapphires and emeralds. It cost Aung a third of his wealth.

Mala took one look, pushed it away and said not a word.

Aung was heartbroken. The next morning, he decided to find Mala's father and help him. Maybe then, she would forgive him.

But the ogre and the sorcerer advised him against it. 'Besides,' they said, 'Mala ran away last night.'

In despair, Aung now turned to the holy hermit for the first time.

'You imagined that wealth brings happiness. But what is important is not what you have but what you do with it.'

Aung realised his mistake. From that day, he used his wealth to do good. He built a **pagoda**, and offered food and shelter to all visitors.

One day, Aung saw a woman he knew well. An older man stood beside her, both of them wearing **humble** clothes.

'Mala!' cried Aung. He rushed over to them and knelt before her puzzled father.

'Sir, I have done you great wrong. I beg your forgiveness. All I have, I give it up gladly. I will be content to return to my village and make puppets.'

'Father,' said Mala softly, 'this is Aung. But he has changed!'[1]

'So it would seem!' said her father. 'If so, it would be a shame to let him go. Perhaps, he would like to work for me.'

So Aung became the merchant's assistant and when Mala's heart was won, his son-in-law.

Aung still called on the puppets. But though he was helped often by strength and knowledge, he was guided always by wisdom and goodness.

pagoda: a temple in the form of a tower with multiple levels

humble: (here) ordinary

Literary term

1. This is an example of **exclamation**. Here, Mala is using it to express feelings of joy and surprise.

About the author

Aaron Shepard (1950–) is an American children's author. He specialises in retelling folktales and other traditional literature from around the world. Some of his published works are *The Legend of Lightning Larry, The Monkey King: A Superhero Tale of China* and *The Magic Flyswatter: A Superhero Tale of Africa*.

Comprehension

Quick Recap

A. Answer these questions in a few lines.

1. Why did Aung not want to be a puppet maker?
2. What did the king of the god represent and what advice did he give to Aung?
3. Which puppet helped Aung in gaining the riches of the caravan? How?

4. What did Aung gift Mala?
5. What advice did the holy hermit give to Aung when Mala ran away?

B. Read the lines from the story and answer the questions.

1. *'The life of a puppet maker is an honourable one. But if you must go, let me give you companions for your journey.'*
   a. Who said this and to whom?
   b. Who wanted to leave? Why?
   c. Which companions is the speaker talking about?

2. *'I'll take you with me and care for you.'*
   a. Who said this and to whom?
   b. How did the speaker meet the listener?
   c. What was the listener's reaction to this?

Life Skills and Values

overcoming greed

Think and answer.

1. Do you think all the four virtues guided Aung in the right direction? Why/Why not?
2. In your opinion, which virtue is the most important and why?
3. How did Aung's good deeds help him? Do you think he learned from his mistakes?

Way with Words

Phrasal Verbs

A. Match the phrasal verbs with their meanings.

A	B
1. carry on	a. live in one place
2. find out	b. arrive unexpectedly
3. get along	c. continue
4. settle down	d. start a journey
5. turn up	e. learn, discover
6. set off	f. like being with

B. Use the following phrasal verbs to complete the sentences.

grows up	gave up	carried on	try on	broke down	believe in

1. Many children still ____________ Santa Claus.
2. She ____________ on hearing the news of the loss.
3. He ____________ junk food because it was harmful for his health.
4. The party ____________ till well past midnight.
5. Meeta wants to become a pilot when she ____________.
6. I want to ____________ those shoes.

Grammar in Use

TYPES OF ADJECTIVES

Adjectives are words that describe nouns or pronouns.

Look at this table which shows the different types of adjectives.

Type of Adjective	Example
Adjectives of Quality tell us the kind or quality of a person or a thing.	Aung now turned to the **holy** hermit for the first time.
Adjectives of Quantity tell us the quantity of things.	Please give me **some** milk.
Adjectives of Number tell us the number of things or persons there are.	He showed his son the **four** wooden puppets that he had made.
Demonstrative Adjectives tell us which person or thing we are referring to.	'**This** place looks like a good place to sleep,' he said to himself.
Possessive Adjectives show possession or belonging.	It cost Aung a third of **his** wealth.
Interrogative Adjectives are used before nouns to ask questions.	At **what** time does the train depart?

A. Underline the adjectives in these sentences and state their types.

1. Reitesh won the second prize in the race.
2. Which bag do you prefer?
3. Our teacher told us a very nice story.

4. He has lost all his wealth.
5. The foolish crow tried to sing a song.
6. This girl dances quite well.
8. The friendly atmosphere in the hotel makes it a nice place to stay in.
9. I saw the accident with my own eyes.
10. Most children like to play cricket.

Types of Prepositions

A **preposition** shows the relation between a noun or a pronoun and some other word in a sentence.

Prepositions are of three types.

Prepositions of time indicate a specific period of time, such as month, date, time and day.

Prepositions of place are used to refer to the place where something or someone is located.

Prepositions of movement show movement from one place to another.

Look at this table which shows the types of prepositions.

Type of Preposition	Example
Time: *on, by, in, at, since, for, before, until* and *till*	He saw a tiger **in** the middle of the night. The music teacher comes **on** Wednesdays. I will meet you **at** 12 p.m.
Place: *in, at, on, by, near, between, beside, behind, in front of* and *under*	He kept the puppets **in** a special room. The palace is **at** the corner of the street. Come and sit **beside** me.
Movement: *to, across, into, around, over, towards* and *along*	The next day took Aung **into** the mountains. He kicked the ball **towards** the goal. We walked **along** the river.

B. Fill in the blanks with the correct prepositions.

1. We saw the man come hurriedly __________ us.
2. Sarah got married __________ the age of twenty-five.
3. The train was travelling __________ 120 kilometres per hour.
4. Please don't be late. Try to be here __________ time.
5. I heard a noise __________ night, but I was too sleepy to check.
6. They put the mirror __________ the wall.
7. We were going __________ Mumbai.
8. He put his hand __________ my bag.

For and Since

> **For** is used for a period of time, and **since** is used to refer to a specific point in time.

Look at the sentences.

I haven't slept well **since** my exams began.

Here, **since** shows a particular point in time in the past to the present time.

I haven't closed my eyes **for** twenty-four hours.

Here, **for** shows a duration or period of time.

C. Complete the sentences using for or since.

1. I've been sitting here __________ three o'clock.
2. How long has it been __________ they left your house?
3. The doctor was available __________ only an hour at his clinic.
4. We have been stranded at the airport __________ nearly five hours.
5. She hasn't slept __________ yesterday because of a stomach ache.
6. I was standing in the queue __________ a very long time.

Study Skills

Pronounce Well

Syllables

> A **syllable** consists of one vowel sound. Syllables make it easy to spell and speak words.

Read the following words aloud.

same	**long**
nose	**jump**

These words have a single vowel sound or syllable.

air-craft	**flo-wer**
doc-tor	**pre-sent**

These words have two vowel sounds or syllables.

for-tu-nate	**do-cu-ment**
for-get-ful	**cus-to-mer**

These words have three vowel sounds or syllables.

Write the number of syllables in the words on the next page. Divide each word by putting a slash (/) after each syllable. One has been done for you.

Example: *dolphin – dol/phin*

1. student
2. fish
3. floating
4. wonderful
5. computer
6. rainbow
7. money
8. April
9. globe
10. distress

Listening and Speaking

Listen to a set of questions and answers. Then form pairs. Take turns to ask and answer questions in the same way.

Pen it Down

21ST CENTURY Media Literacy

Have you ever seen a puppet show? If not, you could watch one on TV or the Internet. Write a short composition about the puppet show.

You can write about:

- the theme of the puppet show
- the story it depicted
- the number of puppets and the characters they played
- how they were dressed
- how you felt

Self Assessment

Now I can

- read and enjoy a Burmese folktale on virtue.
- use phrasal verbs, and use the types of adjectives and prepositions.
- divide words into syllables.
- write a short composition on a given topic.

Read More

The Baker's Dozen: This Christmas tale, retold by Aaron Shepard, is about a baker. It tells the story of how the number thirteen came to be known as 'the baker's dozen'.

Pinocchio: This novel by Carlo Collodi is a story about a puppet who wants to become a real boy. After some hair-raising adventures, his desire is fulfilled.

lyric poem

Seafaring

4

The Fisherman

Abbie Farwell Brown

Let's Get Started

Complete the crossword on words related to fishing.

Across

2. total number of fish caught by someone

4. equipment needed for fishing

7. artificial insect or small fish that is used to attract fish, so that they can be caught

8. baby fish

Down

1. food used to attract fish

3. curved section of strong wire sharpened at one end

5. someone who fishes with a fishing rod, as a hobby

6. a long thin wire or string which is attached to a fishing rod

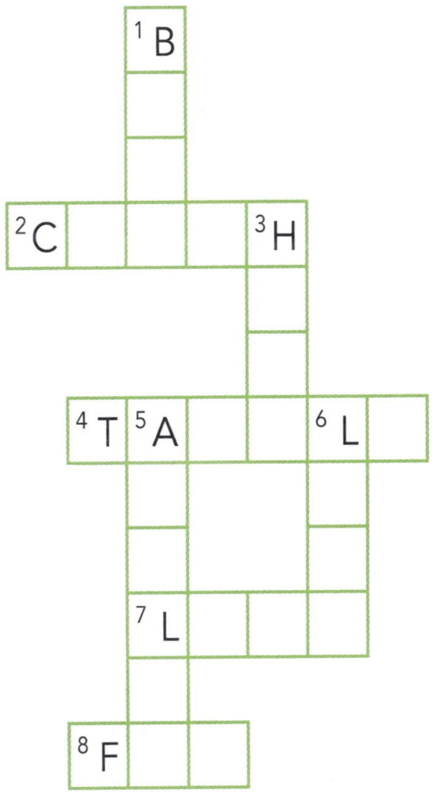

Active Participation: Joy of participation in the collective

Reading

Have you ever seen a fisherman? What type of life do you think a fisherman leads? Read this poem about a fisherman and his life.

The fisherman goes out at dawn
When every one's **abed**,
And from the bottom of the sea
Draws up his daily bread.

His life is strange; half on the shore
And half upon the sea—
Not quite a fish, and yet not quite
The same as you and me.

The fisherman has curious eyes;
They make you feel so **queer**,
As if they had seen many things
Of wonder and of fear.

They're like the sea on foggy days,[1]—
Not gray, nor yet quite blue;
They 're like the **wondrous** tales he tells
Not quite—yet maybe—true.

He knows so much of boats and **tides**,
Of winds and clouds and sky!
But when I tell of city things,
He **sniffs** and shuts one eye!

abed: in bed

queer: (here) strange

wondrous: strange and beautiful

tides: the regular rise and fall in the level of the sea due to the gravitational pull of the moon and the sun

sniffs: (here) expresses contempt or dislike

Literary term

1. This is a **simile**. Here the poet has compared the mystery in the fisherman's eyes to that of the sea on foggy days.

About the poet

Abbie Farwell Brown (1871–1927) was an American author and poet. She published her first children's book *The Book of Saints and Friendly Beasts* in 1900. She started the school newspaper, *The Jabberwock*, when she was a student.

Comprehension

Quick Recap

A. Answer the questions in a few lines.

1. Why does the fisherman go out at dawn?
2. What does the line 'Draws up his daily bread' mean?
3. Why has the poet compared the eyes of the fisherman to the sea on foggy days?
4. Why is Nature of the utmost importance in this poem?

B. Read the lines from the poem and answer the questions.

1. *The fisherman has curious eyes;*
   They make you feel so queer,
   a. Why has the poet used the word 'curious' for the fisherman's eyes?
   b. What do you think the fisherman has seen?
   c. Why do the fisherman's eyes make the poet feel queer?
2. *But when I tell of city things,*
   He sniffs and shuts one eye!
   a. What does the phrase 'sniffs and shuts one eye' tell us about the fisherman's feelings for the city?
   b. Is the poet a city or a countryside dweller? How can you tell?
   c. Do the poet and the fisherman know each other? Give reasons for your answer.

Life Skills and Values

value of hard work

Think and answer.

1. Is the life of a fisherman an easy or a difficult one? Describe the dangers and adventures related to his profession.
2. Do you think the fisherman is happy with his job? Support your answer with three instances from the poem.

21ST CENTURY Productivity

Way with Words

PREFIXES UN-, MIS-

Read this sentence.

The job of a fisherman can be **unsafe** at times and he may have the **misfortune** of running into violent storms at sea.

The words **unsafe** and **misfortune** are made from the words **safe** and **fortune** by adding the prefixes **un-** and **mis-** to them.

A letter or a group of letters that is placed at the beginning of a word is known as a **prefix**.

Examples: **un**educated, **dis**comfort, **mis**interpret

A. Add the prefix mis- or un- to the words given in the box and fill in the blanks using them. Make necessary changes.

understand   lead   well   able   spell   fortune   place   tidy

1. She was ____________ to complete the project despite working hard.
2. People often ____________ his name.
3. The house looked so ____________ after the party was over.
4. The journey ended in ____________ as all the people on the boat were injured.
5. Rubina has a tendency to ____________ valuable belongings.
6. Tina had been ____________ for most of this year, suffering from different ailments.
7. Please do not ____________ my intentions.
8. The media should not ____________ viewers by providing wrong information.

Collocations

Collocation refers to a combination of two or more words that group together quite often in sentences.

Examples: strong smell, heavy rain, great thought, have breakfast

B. Match the words to form collocations.

A	B
1. big	a. fog
2. great	b. surprise
3. large	c. wealth
4. strong	d. population
5. heavy	e. denial

C. Complete the sentences using the collocations from exercise B.

1. The news of her brother's accident came as a ____________ for her.
2. The Sheikh of Abu Dhabi is a man of ____________.

3. Unemployment in the capital is increasing due to the ____________________.
4. The team members were in ____________ of the wrong decision taken by their captain in the cricket match.
5. Many flights got cancelled this winter due to ____________.

D. Underline the correct option in each of these sentences. You may use a dictionary for the meaning of the words, if required.

1. He is *a strict/an ardent/a considerable* fan of David Beckham.
2. This new method is *a significant/a considerable/an unreasonable* advancement in technology.
3. The students do not *take/give/pay* attention in the class.
4. He always takes his boss *with/for/to* granted.
5. It is important to *make/take/give* part in the school's annual function.

Grammar in Use

Subject-verb Agreement

When two subjects are joined by **and**, the verb is plural.

Example: Boats and tides **are** well known by fishermen.

However, when two singular nouns joined by **and** refer to the same person or thing, the verb is singular.

Example: The captain and coach of the team **is** very strict about punctuality.

In case these are two different individuals, two articles are used, and the verb used is plural.

Example: <u>The</u> captain and <u>the</u> coach of the team **are** very strict about punctuality.

If the noun is acting as a unit, we use a singular verb.

Example: The class **is** going for a picnic this afternoon.

If the sentence shows the noun is not used as a unit, we use a plural verb.

Example: The jury **were** divided in their opinion about the guilty verdict.

A. Fill in the blanks with the correct options from the brackets.

1. My brother ______ coming home this weekend. (is/are)
2. I ______ going to Dubai in March. (am/are)
3. Sharif and Hari always ______ their toys with me. (share/shares)
4. Mr Hamid, our teacher and mentor, ______ pleased because we won the quiz. (was/were)
5. Amar ______ two brothers who play tennis as well. (have/has)

6. One of his sisters ______ the guitar. (play/plays)
7. Our coach and art teacher ______ weekend classes as well. (take/takes)
8. My brother and his best friend ______ well. (swim/swims)
9. The students ______ very excited about the upcoming event. (is/are)
10. The committee ______ divided on where to hold the next meeting. (was/were)

Subject and Object Pronouns

You know that pronouns which are used instead of names of people or things are called **personal pronouns**. They can be divided into two categories: subject pronouns and object pronouns.

The **subject** in a sentence is the person or the thing doing something. The **object** is the one to whom something is done.

They can be both nouns and pronouns. When the subject or object of a sentence is a pronoun, they take the following forms.

Person	Singular	Plural
First person	*I, me*	*we, us*
Second person	*you*	*you*
Third person	*he, him, she, her, it*	*they, them*

B. Complete each sentence with the appropriate pronouns from the brackets.

1. Is this cake for me? Yes, it is for ________. (you/her)
2. Neha is hungry, please give ________ some food. (him/her)
3. Here are some seashells. Put ________ in your bag. (them/they)
4. Did anyone see ________ while we were running from the house? (we/us)
5. My brother and ________ went to the market. (I/me)
6. Tina had gone to watch a movie. She liked ________. (that/it)

C. Underline the correct options.

1. Trapti goes to school with *me/I/we/they*.
2. *She/Her/Him/They* is my friend.
3. She is smarter than *they/them/we/he* is.
4. I study as much as *they/them/we/she* does.
5. *They/Them/It/Us* have lost *their* car keys.
6. My friends and *I/me/they/them* are going to play cricket.

Study Skills

Use Your Dictionary

Abbreviations

An **abbreviation** is a shortened form of a long word or phrase.

Example: The abbreviated form of **Member of Parliament** is **MP**.

A. Match the abbreviations with their full forms.

A	B
1. Mr	a. Personal Computer
2. Prof	b. Limited
3. VIP	c. Saint/Street
4. PC	d. Professor
5. St	e. Mister
6. Ltd	f. Very Important Person

B. Write the full forms of the following abbreviations using your dictionary.

1. Dr	4. etc.	7. USA	10. UNO
2. i.e.	5. a.m.	8. p.m.	11. PTO
3. WWF	6. cm	9. UNICEF	12. WHO

Listening and Speaking

A. Listen to these tongue twisters. Repeat these lines several times till you can say them without stumbling or mispronouncing.

She sells seashells on the sea shore.
The shells she sells are surely seashells.
So if she sells shells on the seashore,
I'm sure she sells seashore shells.

Peter Piper picked a peck of pickled peppers,
A peck of pickled peppers Peter Piper picked.
If Peter Piper picked a peck of pickled peppers,
Where's the peck of pickled peppers Peter Piper picked?

B. **Work with a partner and role-play the following situations. Practise making these offers.**

Example: *Student:* Can I get you a glass of water?
Partner: Yes. Thank you!

1. to an old man – help cross the road
2. to a stranger – help find his destination
3. to your teacher – help carry the books
4. to a poor beggar – offer food
5. to your friend – help with class notes
6. to your neighbour – help clean his driveway
7. to your aunt – help look after her dog

Pen it Down

Imagine the life of a fisherman. Write a short composition describing his daily life, both on the shore and at sea.

You can write about:

- how he prepares to go fishing
- when and where he sells his fish
- how much time he spends with his family
- the sights and sounds he enjoys
- the dangers he faces
- how he spends his time with fellow fishermen

Self Assessment

Now I can

- read a poem about the life of a fisherman.
- use prefixes and collocations, understand subject-verb agreement and identify subject and object pronouns.
- say tongue twisters, role-play and make offers to help someone in need.
- write a short composition on a profession.

Read More

Friends: This is a happy and cheerful poem by Abbie Farwell Brown, where she sends a message to children that Nature comforts children in its own way.

Luck: This poem by Abbie Farwell Brown is about the narrator going in search of a four-leaved clover for luck. She turns lucky by finding the right friend.

5 The Birth of the Seasons

Let's Get Started

You have read about Greek and Roman mythology in earlier classes. There are 14 well-known gods and goddesses in Greek mythology. Seven of them are Zeus and his siblings, and the seven others are children of Zeus.

Unjumble the names of these Greek gods and goddesses using the descriptions as clues. Take help from the box to identify their correct names. One has been done for you.

Mercury Athena Ceres Zeus Pluto Mars Apollo Artemis Aphrodite Neptune

usez	king of the hill	*Zeus*
lpuot	god of the underworld and of the dead	______
tpenneu	god of the sea and of earthquakes	______
htaaen	goddess of wisdom and war, and the protector of the city of Athens	______
lolapo	god of the sun, poetry, music and medicine	______
srtimea	goddess of hunting, purity and the moon	______
tiarpehod	goddess of love and beauty	______
rmyeucr	god of science and invention, and the messenger of the gods	______
sarm	god of war	______
eescr	goddess of crops and harvest	______

Learning and Awareness: Coexistence in society and nature

Reading

Do you know why seasons change? Here is a Roman myth about the birth of seasons. Read on to find out how the world was before seasons were born.

Every year, the seasons change as spring gives way to summer, to be followed by autumn and winter. But this was not always so. A very long time ago, when the earth was still young, it was spring all year round. Nature shared her **bounty**[1] and crops grew all through the year.

bounty: large amounts of food or wealth
abode: home
eerie: strange
caverns: large caves
crackled: made repeated short sounds like something is burning in a fire
swooped: seized with a sweeping motion

Literary term

1. This is an example of **personification**. Nature has been treated as a person who shares her bounty and crops.

Jupiter was the king of all Roman gods and lived on Mount Olympus, the **abode** of all the gods. His sister,

Ceres, the goddess of agriculture, was in charge of the harvest. Jupiter, all the gods and mortals worked hard to keep Ceres happy. If she was upset, crops could die. And Ceres was the happiest when she was with her daughter, the beautiful, young goddess, Proserpine. They played together in the fields every day. When Proserpine smiled at her mother, Ceres' heart filled with joy.

While Jupiter ruled the world above, his brother, Pluto was king of the Underworld, a gloomy kingdom far away from the bright world of Olympus. The sun never shone in this dark and **eerie** land with black lakes and dripping **caverns**. The only light was from underground fires, but they never snapped or **crackled**. The waters of the lakes would glow from the light of the silent burning fires.

Pluto loved this world, even if no one else did. He thought it more beautiful than the blue skies, green fields and flowers of the world above. But he had to come to his temples in the world above sometimes, even though the cheery sunlight hurt his eyes and the sweet fragrance of flowers made him feel faint.

It was on one of these visits that Pluto saw Proserpine while she picked flowers in a field, and fell in love with her.

'I have never seen anyone so beautiful,' he thought. 'I will take her home and she will be my queen.' As he **swooped** her up in his chariot, the goddess cried out in surprise and confusion.

Ceres heard her cry from afar. 'My daughter needs my

help,' she cried. But try as she might, she was too far away to come to Proserpine's aid. Pluto rode away, **plunging** his chariot into the darkest depths of the Underworld, taking Proserpine with him.

Her daughter's cry sounding in her heart, Ceres moved across fields, mountains and plains, looking for her.

Filled with anger and grief, she declared, 'Nothing on earth will grow until Proserpine is returned to me. The earth will be **fallow** and crops will die. Famine will destroy all mankind and there will be none to honour the gods.'

It was a dreadful year. It was cold as people had never known before. Oxen pulled the ploughs through **parched**, frozen soil **in vain**, for the earth would not **yield** her riches in return for their labour.

'Will this winter never end?' people asked, as they prayed to the gods to relieve their suffering.

Trapped in Pluto's underworld **realm**, Proserpine knew no way of escaping. Pluto loved her very much, but he would not let her return to her mother.

Though there was no **dearth** of food in the Underworld and Pluto laid out the best food in his kingdom for her, Proserpine would not touch any of it.

'I have never known hunger such as I feel now,' she thought. 'But I dare not eat a **morsel**. For the **Fates** have said that anyone who eats the food of the Underworld can never leave. Even if they do, they will always have to return.'

But as the days went by, Proserpine could not bear her hunger any longer. She ate six pomegranate seeds.

Meanwhile, back on Olympus, Jupiter was worried. If Ceres did not change her decision, the world would be destroyed by famine. Without people to worship the gods, they would lose their importance.

Did You Know? History

A myth is an ancient story which explains natural or historical events. The ancient Greeks and Romans had many common myths.

plunging: jumping or diving quickly and energetically

fallow: uncultivated

parched: dry

in vain: without success

yield: to produce or provide

realm: kingdom

dearth: lack or absence of something

morsel: a small piece or amount of food

Fates: (here) the three sisters who personified destiny, according to Roman mythology

Did You Know? Science

Almost all the planets in our solar system are named after Roman gods and goddesses. Earth is the only planet that is not named after a Roman god or goddess.

compromise: settlement
negotiate: obtain or bring about by discussion
reins: thin leather straps attached round a horse's neck, used to control the horse

Wordwise

The word 'negotiate' has its origin in the Latin word *negotium*. *Neg* means *not* and *otium* means *leisure*. Taken together, it means 'not at leisure'. Gradually, the meaning evolved to mean 'carry on business'.

'A **compromise** is the only way. Ceres won't hear of letting crops grow until Proserpine returns to her. And I know Pluto. He will never agree to let her go.'

So, Jupiter did what he often did. He sent his youngest son, Mercury, the messenger god, to **negotiate** a deal with Pluto.

Even as a child, Mercury had been clever at making deals. But this deal might be his hardest yet. Pluto, king of the Underworld, was deeply in love with Proserpine.

When Mercury heard that Proserpine had eaten the pomegranate seeds, he had to think quickly.

'My lord,' he said to Pluto, 'I am here by Jupiter's command. Proserpine must return to the world above, for Ceres has sworn to lay the whole world to waste if she does not return. However, she will not be away from you forever.'

The deal Mercury made with Pluto was that Proserpine would live as queen of the Underworld for six months of the year. However, each spring, she would return and live with her mother on earth for the other six months.

Pluto agreed. Proserpine agreed too.

Mercury took the **reins** of Pluto's chariot and took Proserpine to the upper world where her mother waited. Ceres was overjoyed to be reunited with her daughter. She took back her threat, to Jupiter's relief.

In a flash, the world was transformed. The cold winds went away to hide, the grass sprang up and the chirping of birds could be heard once more.

So it is that each spring, Ceres makes the flowers bloom in welcome when her daughter, the Queen of the Underworld, comes to stay with her. Each autumn, when she goes back to Pluto, Ceres cries and lets all the crops die, signalling the start of winter. The next spring, the cycle starts again, when Proserpine returns.

Comprehension

Quick Recap

A. Answer the following questions.

1. What kind of a person was the goddess Ceres? When was she most happy?
2. Where was Pluto from? Describe his kingdom.
3. What did Pluto do after he fell in love with Proserpine?
4. What did Ceres do when Pluto took her daughter away?
5. Why didn't Proserpine eat anything in Pluto's kingdom?

B. Read the lines from the story and answer the questions.

1. *'My daughter needs my help.'*
   a. Who is the speaker here?
   b. Who is the daughter?
   c. What did the speaker do when she couldn't help her daughter?
2. *'I have never known hunger such as I feel now.'*
   a. Who is the speaker here?
   b. Why is she hungry?
   c. What made the speaker feel this way?

Life Skills and Values

understanding relationships

Think and answer.

1. How was Jupiter different from his brother Pluto?
2. What kind of a mother was Ceres? Was her act of destroying the crops and bringing on famine justified?
3. Do you think Mercury was a smart negotiator? Give reasons for your answer.

Way with Words

Antonyms

A. Complete the passage using the antonyms of the words in the brackets.

An elephant is the __________ (smallest) living animal on land. It is quite __________ (tiny) in size. It is usually __________ (bright) grey in colour. Elephants have four legs, and a __________ (short) trunk. The males have two __________ (black) tusks near their trunk. Apart from this, they have two __________ (small) ears and a __________ (long) tail. They are quite social, __________ (foolish) and __________ (useless) animals. Elephants are considered to be __________ (bad) swimmers.

B. In each set of words, underline the word that is opposite in meaning to the rest.

1. admire	respect	praise	punishment
2. attractive	ugly	pretty	pleasing
3. bright	sharp	silly	quick
4. glow	radiate	dull	shine
5. capability	potential	weakness	strength

Grammar in Use

Types of Sentences

You have learned about some of the different types of sentences in previous classes.

An **assertive sentence** states a fact or an opinion. It ends with a full stop (**.**). It can be positive or negative.

An **interrogative sentence** asks a question and ends with a question mark (**?**).

An **exclamatory sentence** expresses a strong feeling or emotion. It has an exclamation mark at the end (**!**).

An **imperative sentence** expresses a command, order, request, advice or suggestion. It ends with a full stop (**.**).

A. Add the correct punctuation mark to each sentence and identify its type.

1. Hurrah We won the match
2. Which dentist did you go to for your toothache
3. We put all our books in this open cupboard
4. Who could have done this terrible thing
5. The driver was driving dangerously fast on the highway
6. Close the door

7. Let's try this exercise again
8. How clever you are

B. Change each sentence according to the instructions given in the brackets.

1. He has no way of getting out of the situation. (change to interrogative)
2. It is very hot in Delhi today. (change to exclamatory)
3. Is it a good idea to start so late for the show? (change to assertive)
4. Father baked a delicious cake. (change to exclamatory)
5. Rahel has never gone to the museum. (change to interrogative)

Abstract Nouns

An **abstract noun** refers to an idea, a quality, an action or a state. Abstract nouns refer to things which are not concrete, that is, with which we cannot interact physically.

Abstract nouns can be formed from other words, such as adjectives, verbs and common nouns.

Examples: happy → happiness jealous → jealousy

C. Complete the sentences using abstract nouns formed from the words given in the brackets.

1. Hercules was known for his great ____________. (strong)
2. The people in this part of the state live in ____________. (poor)
3. ____________ should always be controlled. (angry)
4. ____________ is next to godliness. (clean)
5. ____________ is the best policy. (honest)

Study Skills

Spell Check

Complete these words with the letters given in the brackets. In some words, you may have to use the letters more than once.

1. casua____y (l)
2. o____ered (f)
3. interes____ing (t)
4. ha____ening (p)
5. hu____ying (r)
6. di____erent (f)

Listening and Speaking

Listen to the words and write them under the season which they are related to.

Spring	Summer	Autumn	Winter

Pen it Down

The story 'The Birth of the Seasons' has been written in the third person (he). Rewrite the story in brief in the first person (I), from the viewpoint of Jupiter.

You may begin like this:

I live on Mount Olympus and my sister Ceres is in charge of the harvest ...

HC Potential to understand

Self Assessment

Now I can

- read and enjoy a mythological story related to the origin of seasons.
- use antonyms, identify different types of sentences and form abstract nouns.
- identify missing letters in words and write a story from a different viewpoint.

Read More

Pandora's Box: This story from Greek mythology centres around the first woman on earth, Pandora, and what happens when she opens the box presented to her.

The Mighty Hercules: This story from Greco-Roman mythology is about the brave warrior Hercules, son of Zeus. His bravery earned him a place at Mount Olympus, the abode of the gods.

6

Roving on the Red Planet

Let's Get Started

Read some interesting facts about various man-made objects related to space and use the help box to complete the sentences.

International Space Station

Hubble Space Telescope

Mir Space Station

GPS

weather satellite

automobiles	energy	temperatures	Japan	wheat

1. The International Space Station was launched on 20 November 1998. It involves the space agencies of the USA, Russia, Europe, Canada and ______________.
2. The Hubble Space Telescope gets ______________ from the sun using two 25-foot solar panels. It is about the size of a large school bus.
3. Mir was the first modular space station, i.e., it consisted of multiple separate vehicles that were launched independently. It was assembled in orbit from 1986 to 1996. The first crop of ______________ to be grown from seeds in outer space was in Mir.
4. The GPS (Global Position System) in our mobile phones which gives us location-related information was first introduced for use in ______________ in 1996. It was called Navstar then.
5. Data from weather satellites help us make daily weather forecasts. They tell us about the ______________, wildfires, volcanoes, floods, fog and rising and falling tides.

HC **Learning and Awareness:** Education and Knowledge

Reading

Do you wish to go to Mars? Read about the various scientific missions launched in the hope that one day humans can also visit the planet.

Touchdown!

'Touchdown **confirmed**! *Perseverance* is safely on the surface of Mars, ready to begin seeking the signs of past life.'

Dr Swati Mohan's voice held quiet excitement as she made the announcement to the world on 18 February 2021. Mohan was the Indian-American scientist in charge of NASA's (National Aeronautics and Space Administration) landing of its *Perseverance* rover on the red planet.

confirmed: proven to be true
shield: a protective cover
withstand: remain unaffected by
stunning: very impressive
tracking: following something
muffled: not very clear

Perseverance was a spacecraft which had been launched in 2020. The size of an SUV, it had a robotic arm for picking up and storing rock samples, and a heat **shield** that let it **withstand** temperatures up to 1315 degree Centigrade.

Travelling through space for seven months, the *Perseverance* had arrived at the moment celebrated by scientists and space lovers alike. It landed near a huge crater which held the remains of what looked like river deltas.

Within seconds of landing, *Perseverance* – which was the forty-ninth expedition to Mars – sent back two **stunning** images of its new home. Eighteen hours later, it recorded and sent back the sounds of Martian wind. It may not have amounted to much for most people, but to the scientists **tracking** the rover's every move, the **muffled** sound was

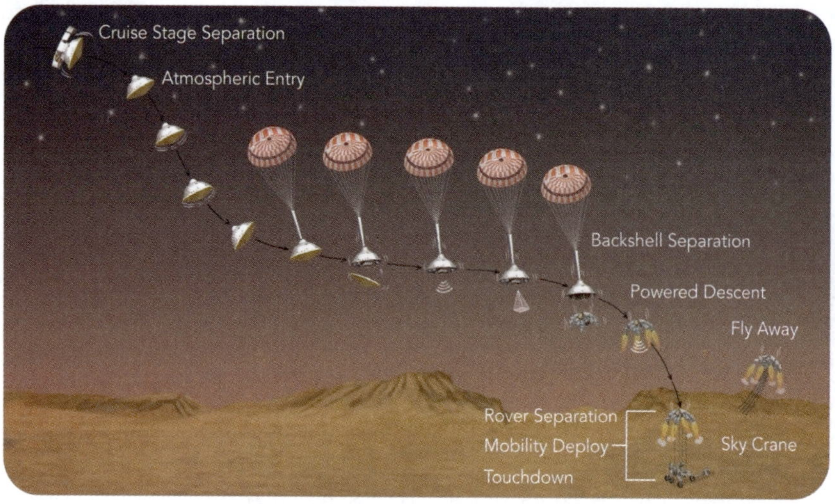

Perseverance landing on Mars

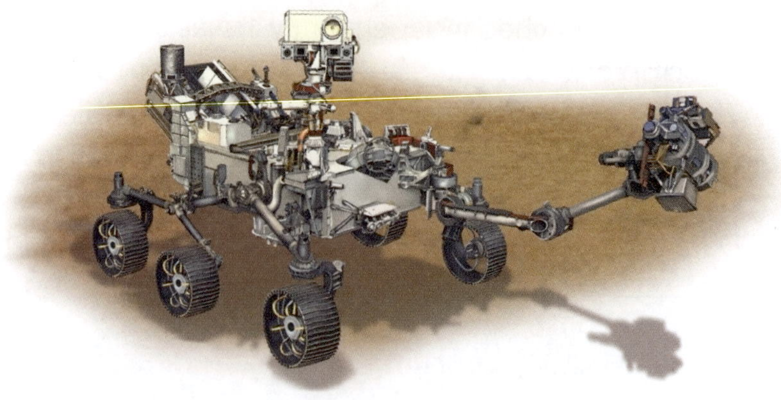

The *Perseverance* rover

'sweet symphony', like 'listening to a seashell, or having a hand cupped over the ear.'

Why are human beings so curious about the red planet, so called because of the loose red layer of dust and minerals that covers it like a blanket? In many ways, Mars is similar to our own planet, to which it is a **cosmic** neighbour, though separated by a distance of 305.75 million kilometres.

In stories of science fiction, one of the most common ideas is that of **galactic** travel and of humans setting up **colonies** on Mars. In many of these stories, Mars is **inhabited** by **aliens** who look partly like humans, with thin bodies and giant heads. But in real life, these are the questions driving scientists:

Does Mars have water on it? If it does, does it also have life on it? Or, did it have some kind of life once and then everything disappeared?

The first 360-degree panorama taken by *Perseverance*

This is why scientists look for signs of **microscopic** life forms that may have once lived on this planet with two moons that is half the size of Earth.

'Dare Mighty Things'

Perseverance landed on Mars with the help of a parachute which carried a secret message. Written in computer code, it was, 'Dare Mighty Things'. The rover's achievements have repeatedly upheld this motto. One of these is the mini helicopter, *Ingenuity*, which the rover had carried. *Ingenuity*, whose name was selected through a high school writing competition won by Indian American Vaneeza Rupani, is an experimental aircraft. Its purpose was to prove that an aircraft could

Science fiction often imagines aliens with thin bodies and giant heads living on Mars

Did You Know? Science

The layer of dust and minerals which covers Mars has a lot of iron oxide, a substance present in our blood and in rusted iron vessels. If an iron bucket filled with water is left out in the sun for a month, it will turn into the same shade!

cosmic: related to the cosmos or the universe

galactic: related to a galaxy, or a system of stars in outer space, containing suns and their planets

colonies: groups of people living in a foreign place

inhabited: lived in

aliens: creatures from another world

microscopic: too small to be visible to the naked eye

Ingenuity, the mini helicopter transported to Mars on *Perseverance*

fly on another planet and send back flight information to Earth. After fulfilling its purpose, *Ingenuity*, designed by another Indian American, Bob Balaram, was to have stayed where it was, while *Perseverance* drove away on its own journey. But the tiny helicopter performed so well that NASA has decided that it would stay and help *Perseverance* gather information.

Who designed *Ingenuity*?

After *Ingenuity*, the rover soon added another feather in its cap. On 27 April 2021, the special 'MOXIE' tool in *Perseverance* was able to produce oxygen out of the thin Martian air! Like a tree on Earth, MOXIE inhaled carbon dioxide and produced oxygen. It produced 10 grams of oxygen from the carbon dioxide in Mars' atmosphere, which would let an astronaut breathe for 10 minutes. So long, astronauts had to carry their own oxygen for space missions, adding greatly to the spacecraft's weight. Rockets also use oxygen as fuel. MOXIE's **feat** gives hope that future travellers headed to Mars can use this technology not only to breathe but also to power their rockets back to Earth.

feat: achievement

resembled: looked like

gravity: the force which causes things to drop to the ground

flyby: a spacecraft that flies close past a heavenly body, gathering information to send back to the Earth.

Hello, Neighbour!

Mars gets its name from the Roman god of war. Ancient civilizations around the world were interested in astronomy and the ancient Romans associated the planet with war because its red colour **resembled** the colour of blood.

Today, we know that the **gravity** of Mars is a third of that of Earth. This means that on Mars, you could jump over your car to the other side instead of walking around it! When NASA sent *Mariner 4*, its first spacecraft to Mars, in 1964, they designed it keeping this in mind. It was a **flyby** mission.

Mars, the Roman god of war

A day on Mars is almost as long as a day on Earth. A Martian year, however, has about 687 days. Every 26 months, Earth and Mars come very close to each other, lining up in a straight line. This is when most of the Mars missions have been **launched**. Even at this distance, travelling to Mars takes close to eight months!

The first rover to land on Mars was the little bread box-sized robot, *Prop-M*. Sent in 1971 by Russia (then USSR), it survived less than two minutes. It was not until 1996 that the USA successfully sent the *Sojourner* to Mars. The success encouraged NASA to send more rovers. Of these, *Curiosity*, sent in 2011, continues to send back valuable data.

launched: set in motion

barren: land that is not fertile

expeditions: journeys undertaken for a specific purpose

unravel: solve

How many days are there in a Martian year?

The only other country to successfully land a rover on Mars is China, whose *Zhurong* rover entered Mars' orbit on 10 February 2021. India had sent its first successful orbiter *Mangalyaan* to Mars in 2013 to test its own rocket launching system.

Signs of Life

Mars is a cold, **barren** land with dust storms lasting months. However, the images sent by the rovers show signs of flowing water, raising hopes of finding signs of past life.

The **expeditions** confirm that water once flowed in Mars. It has minerals which would not have been formed if moisture weren't there.

Perhaps in another 25 years, human beings will walk on Mars. Maybe we would grow plants on the barren planet and make it more suitable for human life. When the ancient Romans were naming their planets, little did they know that many centuries later, people would send hi-tech spacecraft to other heavenly bodies! Science has helped us **unravel** many mysteries. It continues to give us hope to dream of bigger things.

Comprehension

Quick Recap

A. Answer the questions in a few lines.

1. Who is Dr Swati Mohan?
2. Describe what *Perseverance* looks like.
3. How is Mars often shown in science fiction stories?
4. What are some of the questions about Mars that drive scientists?
5. What do we know about Mars' gravity?

6. When are most of the Mars missions launched?
7. Write the story behind the planet's name and the reason why it is called the 'red planet'.
8. What are some of the other spacecrafts which have reached Mars?

B. Read the lines from the passage and answer the questions.

1. *The rover's achievements have repeatedly upheld this motto.*
   a. What motto is being spoken about in the above line? Where was this 'motto' found?
   b. What are two of the rover's achievements?
   c. What was the role of two Indian Americans in these achievements?
2. *Eighteen hours later, it recorded and sent back the sounds of Martian wind.*
   a. What did the scientists compare the sounds of Martian wind with?
   b. What had happened eighteen hours ago? Describe the event.
   c. What else had *Perseverance* sent back after landing?

Life Skills and Values importance of space exploration

Think and answer.

1. If you were an astronaut travelling to Mars, would you take the *Ingenuity* or MOXIE with you? Give reasons for your answer.
2. Why do you think that space exploration is important?

Way with Words

Contextual Usage

A. Read the clues and solve the crossword puzzle.

Across

1. also known as the red planet
2. a large bowl-shaped hole in the ground
3. a creative piece of music
4. belonging to the very distant past

Down

5. creatures from other worlds
6. a person who is an expert in the field of science
7. pictures or photographs
8. the study of celestial objects

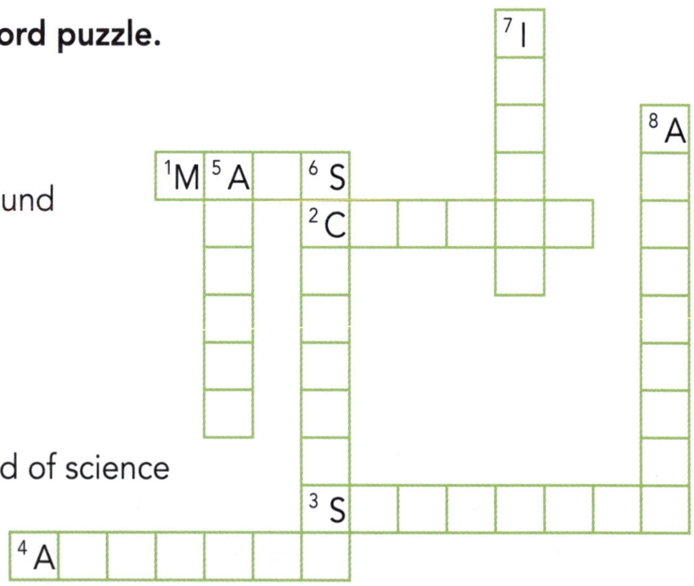

Words Related to Space

B. Fill in the blanks with the given words related to space.

astronaut	comet	star	galaxy	orbit	eclipse	planet

1. The Earth goes around the sun along its ____________.
2. When the ____________ returned to Earth after a successful mission, he was greeted with shouts of praise.
3. During a solar ____________, we should avoid looking at the sun with our naked eyes.
4. Our ____________ is called the Milky Way.
5. I was amazed by the sight of a falling ____________.
6. Mercury is the smallest ____________ in the solar system.
7. A small object that goes around the sun and has a long tail of gas is called a __________.

Measures of Uncountable Nouns

Read the sentence.

The images sent by the rovers show signs of flowing **water**.

'Water' is an uncountable noun and it does not have a plural form. But, uncountable nouns can be measured when used with measure words.

Example: Ahmed packed **three bottles of water** for the journey across the desert.

C. Complete the sentences using suitable measure words from the box.

cubes	drop	cups	pinch	glass

1. I would like three ____________ of sugar in my tea.
2. I drink a ____________ of milk every day.
3. He bought two ____________ of coffee.
4. There is not even a ____________ of water in the house.
5. Add only a ____________ of salt to the salad.

Grammar in Use

Present continuous Tense

Read these sentences.

Perseverance **is seeking** the signs of past life on Mars now.

The special tool **is producing** oxygen out of the thin Martian air.

The words in bold tell us that the action is happening in the present.

In the **present continuous tense**, the verb shows an action in the present which is happening at the time of speaking.

The present continuous tense is also used for:

1. Temporary situations, when we feel something will not continue for a long time.
   Example: She **is staying** with her friend for a week.
2. Definite future arrangements (with a future time word) where something is certain to happen in the future.
   Example: I **am meeting** my grandfather tomorrow.
3. Talking about a situation which is slowly changing.
   Example: I **am getting** better at playing table tennis.

A. Fill in the blanks with the present continuous tense of the given verbs.

1. We ______________ (go) to see the film later today.
2. They ______________ (bring) the cake for the party.
3. We ______________ (meet) your friend at four in the evening.
4. Winter ______________ (not end) this year.
5. Shubhra and Mita ______________ (play) the piano.
6. Mukul ______________ (ride) his bicycle in the evening.

Past Continuous tense

The **past continuous tense** describes an action that was taking place at a particular moment in the past. The action started before that moment and had not finished by that moment.

Example: When the scientist heard the sounds of Martian wind, he felt that he **was listening** to a seashell.

The past continuous is made from the past tense of the verb **be** and the **-ing** form of a verb.

B. Fill in the blanks with the past continuous tense of the given verbs.

walk	help	have	watch	play	sing

1. My friend and I ______________ badminton when it started raining.
2. We ______________ dinner when the doorbell rang.
3. They ______________ a T20 match when their guests arrived.
4. As I ______________ down the road, I saw an accident take place.
5. When I entered my parents' room, they ______________ a duet.
6. When the earthquake struck, Rahil ______________ me with my project.

Forming Wh- Questions

You know that the wh- question words are **why, how, what, when, where, who, whom, which** and **whose**.

Read this sentence and the question framed for it.

Perseverance recorded the sounds of Martian wind.

What sounds did *Perseverance* record?

C. Frame questions for the given answers using wh- question words.

1. My aunt lives in Chandigarh.
2. Suresh watched the *Harry Potter* film at the theatre.
3. Sujatha sprained her leg last week.
4. Sadiq is not going to the party because he has an exam tomorrow.
5. The girl with the red bag is my sister.

Study Skills

Spell Check

Words Ending with -ar and -er

A. Look at the spelling of these words carefully. Say them aloud and notice the way they sound the same.

solar better after beggar container grammar calendar

B. Complete these words with -ar or -er.

1. burgl __ __
2. labour __ __
3. famili __ __
4. knitwe __ __
5. administ __ __
6. barb __ __
7. muscul __ __
8. bowl __ __
9. pill __ __
10. bright __ __

Listening and Speaking

In pairs, enact an imaginary conversation between an astronaut who has travelled to Mars and her/his friend speaking over satellite phone, in the year 2030.

You can use the words and phrases given in the box and begin with the lines below.

source of life important discovery footprints bubbling stream large craters floating around living in a spaceship lonely

Astronaut: You wouldn't believe what I have just discovered!

Friend: Tell me quickly. I am keen to know what you have found.

Pen it Down

A. Imagine that you are the Mars rover that was sent on the expedition. Write an autobiographical account of your experience on Mars.

You can include the following points:

- The preparation for the journey
- Landing safely on Mars
- Achievements and milestones
- Hopes for the future

B. Your school is organising an essay writing contest. The topic for the essay is 'Why I Want to Go to Space'. The first two winners of the contest will receive the chance to visit NASA's Kennedy Space Center in Florida, USA. Write a notice announcing the contest.

Keep the following points in mind:

- Mention the date, time and venue for the contest.
- Your notice should have a catchy title related to the event.
- The date of the event must be about two weeks after the announcement.

Self Assessment

Now I can

- read and understand a passage about the Mars rover, *Perseverance*.
- complete a crossword, use words related to space and measures of uncountable nouns.
- understand the usage of past and present continuous tenses and form *wh-* questions.
- spell words ending with *-ar* and *-er*, and carry out a conversation on a given topic.
- write an autobiographical account and a notice.

Read More

An Astronaut's Diary: This story by Satyajit Ray describes the experiences of scientist and inventor, Professor Shonku, as he journeys to Mars, where he is attacked by Martians, and flees to another friendly planet.

The Girl who Named Pluto: This is the story of eleven-year-old Venetia Burney who decided that the ninth major planet – which was discovered but was yet to be named – might be called Pluto.

Be Creative!

A. The story 'The Birth of the Seasons' talks about two seasons – spring and winter. The other seasons are summer and autumn. The famous British poet P. B. Shelley described autumn in the following words:

I love all that you love,
Spirit of delight;
The fresh earth in new leaves dressed,
And the starry night;
Autumn evening and the morn
When the golden mists are born.

Find out at least eight words related to autumn. Write them in the lines below. Then, next to each, write as many rhyming words as you can think of. The first two are done for you.

Autumn Words	Rhyming Words
1. *gold*	*bold, hold, fold, cold, scold, sold*
2. *fall*	*ball, mall, call, hall, wall, tall*
3. ________	____________________
4. ________	____________________
5. ________	____________________
6. ________	____________________
7. ________	____________________
8. ________	____________________

B. You read about the planet Mars in the chapter 'Roving on the Red Planet.' Divide the class into two groups and do the following activity.

Hold a debate in class with the motion: 'Humans should improve life on Earth rather than wasting resources on missions to Mars'. Ask the teacher to call out five students randomly from each group to speak either *for* or *against* the motion. Let them speak and debate on the topic while maintaining decorum in class. Invite your teacher to judge the debate and announce if the motion is passed or not, based on the arguments presented. Give a big round of applause for the speakers!

7 The Secret Cavern

Margaret Widdemer

Let's Get Started

Most of the time, we enjoy the company of our friends and family. However, there are also times when we like to be on our own, reading, thinking or just daydreaming.

Match these expressions about dreams in column A with their meanings in column B.

Expression	Meaning
1. beyond your wildest dreams	a. to have imaginary, pleasant thoughts
2. dream come true	b. when something is unlikely to happen
3. pipe dream	c. when something broken works better once repaired
4. daydream about something	d. when the results exceed one's expectations
5. in your dreams	e. what you really wished for has come true
6. works like a dream	f. a goal that is impossible to reach
7. broken dreams	g. would not even consider doing something
8. wouldn't dream of doing it	h. wishes or desires that didn't come true

HC **Active Participation:** Desiring prosperity

Reading

Do you have a secret hideout of your own? In this poem, the speaker is a child who has her own secret place. What does she keep there? Read the poem to find out how she uses it.

Underneath the **boardwalk**, way, way back,
There's a splendid cavern, big and black—
If you want to get there, you must crawl
Underneath the posts and steps and all
When I've finished **paddling**, there I go—
None of all the other children know!

There I keep my treasures in a box
Shells and coloured glass and queer-shaped rocks,
In a secret hiding place I've made,
Hollowed out with **clamshells** and a spade,
Marked with yellow pebbles in a row
None of all the other children know!

It's a place that makes a splendid **lair**,
Room for chests and weapons and one chair.
In the farthest corner, by the stones,
I shall have a flag with skulls and bones
And a lamp that casts a **lurid** glow
None of all the other children know!

Some time, by and by, when I am grown,
I shall go and live there all alone;
I shall dig and paddle till it's dark,
Then go out and **man** my **pirate bark**:
I shall fill my cave with **captive foe**
None of all the other children know!

boardwalk: a path made of wooden boards, especially on a beach or near water

paddling: (here) walking or wading through shallow water

hollowed: (here) dug

clamshells: shells of clam which have two parts, joined in the middle

lair: hideout; a well-hidden place

lurid: very brightly coloured, often creating an unnatural and unpleasant effect

man: to work and be in charge of a place

pirate bark: a small sailing vessel propelled by oars or sails

captive: kept as a prisoner

foe: enemy

About the poet

Margaret Widdemer (1884–1978) was an American poet and novelist. She won the Pulitzer Prize for her collection of poems *The Old Road to Paradise* in 1919. *Little Girl and Boy Land* and *Hill Garden* are some of the other books she had written.

Wordwise

The word 'pirate' comes from the Latin word *pirata*, which means 'sea robber'.

Comprehension

Quick Recap

A. Answer the questions in a few lines.

1. How does the speaker describe the cavern?
2. Why does the speaker wish to live inside the cavern all alone?
3. Why does the speaker do things in a secretive manner? Why doesn't she want anyone else to know?

B. Read the lines from the poem and answer the questions.

1. *There I keep my treasures in a box*
   Shells and coloured glass and queer-shaped rocks
   a. Where does the speaker keep all her treasures?
   b. What all does her treasure include?
   c. How does she keep her treasures safe?
2. *I shall dig and paddle till its dark*
   Then go out and man my pirate bark
   a. What activity will the speaker do till dark?
   b. What is a pirate bark?
   c. What does the speaker plan to do using the pirate bark?

Life Skills and Values

appreciating childhood

Think and answer.

1. Is the speaker a child or a grown-up in this poem? Give reasons for your answer.
2. Do you think the desire to have a secret hiding place is a natural desire? Why or why not?

21ST CENTURY Social Skills

Way with Words

SUFFIX -LY

A **suffix** is used after a word and helps to change its meaning.

The **suffix** *-ly* is used to show 'in what manner'.

Example: He treats people affectionate**ly.**

By adding the suffix *-ly* above, we are able to answer the question, 'In what manner does he treat people?'

A. Match the words in column A with their meanings in column B.

A	B
1. accidental**ly**	a. at an earlier time
2. sufficient**ly**	b. in a truthful manner
3. fluent**ly**	c. occurring twice a year
4. biannual**ly**	d. happening by chance
5. previous**ly**	e. having enough
6. honest**ly**	f. in an effortless manner

B. Complete these sentences with words from the box.

suddenly	comfortably	cruelly	sincerely	faithfully

1. One who is living a stress-free life is living ____________.
2. A person doing work wholeheartedly is working ____________.
3. People who treat animals in an unkind manner, treat them ____________.
4. Dogs show loyalty to their masters and live ____________ with them.
5. When things happen without any warning, they happen ____________.

Grammar in Use

Apostrophe for Plural Possessives

You have learned that the apostrophe (') is used at the end of nouns to show possession. Usually, it is followed by the letter **-s**.

- When singular nouns show possession, we add an **-s** after the apostrophe (').
  Example: Prakash**'s** book
- For plural nouns ending in **-s**, we add only the apostrophe (').
  Example: the student**s'** choice

- For plural nouns not ending in **-s**, we add an **-s** after the apostrophe (').
  Example: people**'s** opinion
- For names ending in **-s**, an apostrophe (') may be added with or without an **-s.**
  Example: Charles**'** house

A. Rewrite the sentences using plural possessives.

1. The name of my friend is Arya.
   My friend's name is Arya.
2. The younger sister of Tina is intelligent.
3. The mothers of my friends walk together daily.
4. The dog of my neighbour barks a lot.
5. The cars of my parents are parked in the garage.
6. The rucksack of Ram looks new.
7. The tyre of my bike is punctured.
8. The name of the hotel down the road is Hotel Broadway.

Apostrophe in Contractions

When a word or a phrase is made shorter by placing an apostrophe (') where the letters are omitted, the new word is called a **contraction**.

Example: he will → he'll

B. Match the contractions with their full forms.

A	B
1. I'm	a. who is
2. aren't	b. will not
3. I've	c. I am
4. they're	d. are not
5. who's	e. I have
6. won't	f. they are

C. Rewrite the sentences using the contractions of the words given in brackets.

1. (We are) going to Mumbai on Sunday.
2. (Who will) stay at your house when you go to Mumbai?
3. We (should not) throw garbage on the road.

4. I (can not) accompany you because I (have not) finished my homework.
5. I think (it is) going to rain heavily tonight.
6. I think (they are) very nice boys.

INTERJECTIONS

Read this sentence.

Hurrah! We won the match.

Words like **wow**, **hurrah**, **ouch** and **alas** are **interjections**. They express the feelings or emotions of the speaker. They are always followed by an exclamation mark.

D. Complete the sentences with the correct interjections. Remember to add exclamation marks.

Bravo	Oh no	Hurrah	Oh dear	Alas	Well done

1. ______________ Our school won the competition.
2. ______________ She fell down and broke her leg.
3. ______________ You have scored the highest marks.
4. ______________ I have lost my wallet.
5. ______________ You played very well.
6. ______________ Nelson Mandela is no more.

Study Skills

Spell Check

A. Make new words by adding -ing to these words. Notice how the spelling changes.

1. travel 2. bake 3. visit 4. admit 5. try 6. excite

B. Correct the following sentences by using words ending in -ing.

1. It was disappointed for my son to miss the match.
2. After a terrified car accident, everyone was in a shock.
3. I am starting a new course next week. It sounds excitement.
4. 'I like being old', said the man with a satisfy grin.
5. She learns fast. She is making amazement progress.
6. My mother is make noodles for breakfast.

Listening and Speaking

Listen to your teacher read out pairs of words. Now, repeat each pair of words twice. Write these words.

You will notice that in each word, there are certain consonants without a vowel in between them.

Example: In the words, **spray** and **spring**, the letters **spr** have no vowels in between them.

Identify other such letters in each of the words.

Pen it Down

Draw and colour a picture of a sea beach. Describe your picture.

You could draw and describe:

- a sea and brown sand next to it
- a bright sun in the blue sky
- seagulls flying in the sky
- some palm trees and huts on the beach
- children making sandcastles
- some seashells and pebbles
- a fishing boat in the sea

HC Creative self-expression

Self Assessment

Now I can

- read a poem about the secret dreams of a child.
- understand the usage of the suffix *-ly* and make new words by adding *-ing*.
- use the apostrophe for possessives and contractions.
- practise interjections and draw and describe a scene.

Read More

Garden Dream: This poem is a part of a collection of poems by Margaret Widdemer in her book *An Old Road to Paradise.*

When I was a Young Girl: This is another poem by Margaret Widdemer about an adult looking back at a time when she was a young girl.

folktale

8

The Barber's Wife

Romila Thapar

Let's Get Started

Do you know about Community Watch? It is a concept in which the people of a locality take turns to keep watch and protect the community from thieves and intruders. Since the police cannot be everywhere at all times, this is a great way to keep communities safe and build a strong bond among the people of the neighbourhood. However, there are many dos and don'ts when it comes to Community Watch.

Read these guidelines and add a tick [✓] next to the ones you think are related to Community Watch.

1. If you notice a strange car parked near your house for a long time, notify us. ☐
2. Come to the community hall on Sunday to discuss the plan for Independence Day celebrations. ☐
3. When you see a thief, catch him yourself and turn him over to the police. ☐
4. When you leave town, let one of your neighbours know so that they can check around your house for any suspicious activity. ☐
5. Bring something delicious to the next neighbourhood potluck and show off your cooking skills. ☐
6. Water your plants and clean your yard regularly to maintain the greenery of the neighbourhood. ☐

Learning and Awareness: Clarity of purpose

Reading

Can wit and intelligence change a person's fortune? This is a story about a barber's wife

who got into many difficult situations. Find out how she saved herself each time.

There was once a very **clumsy** barber. The poor man could never cut someone's hair without cutting off a bit of his ear or shave a man without leaving **gashes** on his face. Few people came to him, and his family was extremely poor.

One day, the barber waited all day for customers, but no one came. His wife was very angry when he went home empty-handed. 'There is nothing for us to eat tonight. I wanted to buy some food, but you tell me that you have made nothing all day,' she said. As she stamped out of the room, she cried, 'If you can't earn money, then go and beg for some.'

The barber thought this was a good idea. The king was getting married that day and would be sure to be generous to his people. He set off for the palace. At the palace, he bowed respectfully to the king and begged him to give him something.

The king was amused and ordered his minister to grant the barber some wasteland outside the city.

The barber returned home delighted.

'Well,' asked his wife, 'what did the king give you?'

clumsy: not skillful

gashes: long, deep wounds or cuts

imitate: copy the way someone does something

startled: surprised

Wordwise

The word 'barber' is derived from the Latin word *barba*, which means beard. In olden times, the main work of barbers was to trim beards.

'Some land outside the city,' he replied.

'Oh, you foolish man!' she exclaimed. 'Since when have you become a farmer, asking for a piece of land? What are we going to do with it?'

When her anger had cooled a little, they went to see the land. It was a large patch of uneven ground. The woman shrank with horror at the thought of the work they would have to put into ploughing the land before they could plant anything on it.

But she was never without an idea for long. She ordered her husband to **imitate** her movements and soon they were both walking slowly over the land, their eyes on the ground, as if looking for something.

A band of robbers was passing that way. Their leader approached the wife and asked her if they had lost something. She pretended to be **startled** and said, 'Oh no, nothing at all.'

When the robber insisted, she took him aside and said, 'My uncle died a week ago. Before he died, he told me that he had buried five pots of gold in this field. We are trying to find them. But you must promise not to tell anyone.'

The robber swore that he wouldn't and left. Soon the barber and his wife returned home. The wife was **in high spirits**. When the two went back to the field the next morning, every inch of it had been dug. The barber's wife **chuckled** as she explained what had happened. 'I knew the robber would tell his friends what he had heard. The poor things must have spent all night digging up the field to find the gold. Now, all we have to do is plant some grain.'

She bought grain **on credit** from the corn merchant and planted it. The harvest was **magnificent**, for the land had been dug well. The barber's wife sold the crop for a large sum and they started living in comfort.

in high spirits: happy and excited

chuckled: laughed quietly

on credit: on an arrangement that payment can be made at a later date

magnificent: very good

sore: angry and upset

revenge: something you do to hurt or punish someone who has hurt or harmed you

garbage: waste material

But the robbers were very **sore** about being cheated by the barber's wife. They waited for an opportunity to take **revenge**. One evening, as it was getting dark, their leader slipped into the barber's house and hid himself. But the barber's wife saw him. She went into the kitchen, took a shallow bowl and filled it with **garbage**. On top, she put a layer of sweets. Then, she whispered to her husband that as soon as she was in bed, he must ask her in a loud voice where she had put the money.

A few minutes later, the barber came into their room and asked, 'Where have you put the money? I hope it is in a safe place.'

His wife replied, 'Don't worry. I have put it at the bottom of the bowl which has the sweets. No one will ever find it.'

The robber smiled and waited until the two were asleep. Then, he crept into the kitchen and made off with the bowl of sweets. You can imagine how angry the robbers were when all they found in the bowl was kitchen garbage under a layer of sweets. They swore that they would not rest easy until they had robbed the barber's wife of the money.

When summer set in, the days were hot and the nights were cool. It was more pleasant to sleep **outdoors** than in a room. So the barber and his wife put their beds in the backyard, where the cool night breeze brought on a deep sleep.

outdoors: outside the house

palanquin: a box-like structure with poles fixed on opposite sides, used to carry people in olden days

crouched: lowered the body by bending the knees completely

hollow: (here) deep and echoing

scared out of their wits: extremely frightened

leisurely: without haste or hurry

That night, the barber's wife dreamt that she was riding in a **palanquin**. It was very pleasant indeed. She opened her eyes. To her surprise, she realised that she wasn't in a palanquin at all. Instead, her bed was being carried away by the robbers.

'What shall I do?' she thought. 'I really have been trapped this time. I can't expect mercy from them now.'

Then, she heard one of them say, 'She is so heavy. My shoulder is beginning to hurt. Let's put the bed down for a while.' They placed the bed under a banyan tree, laid down and dozed off.

The woman knew this was her chance to escape. She arranged the bedclothes so that it appeared that she was asleep. Then, she climbed up on the tree. She bundled herself up and **crouched** on a thick branch.

Just as the robbers began waking up, she began howling in a **hollow** voice. In the silence and darkness, the sound was terrifying. She had wrapped her face and arms in her white shawl, and now, let the ends flap. The robbers saw a white figure sitting on the tree, flapping its wings and howling. They were certain that it was a ghost and that the tree was haunted.

Scared out of their wits, the robbers took to their heels. The barber's wife could hardly stop laughing. She climbed down from the tree **leisurely**, picked up her bed and walked home.

The robbers were never heard of in the neighbourhood again.

About the author

Romila Thapar (1931–) is one of the most well-known Indian historians. Her famous books include *A History of India*, *Aśoka and the Decline of the Maurya* and *Early India: From the Origins to AD 1300*.

Comprehension

Quick Recap

A. Answer the questions in a few lines.

1. Why was the barber's wife angry with him?
2. Why was the barber gifted a piece of land?
3. Why was the barber's wife not happy with the king's gift to her husband?
4. How did the barber's wife trick the band of robbers?
5. How did the robbers try to take revenge on the barber's wife?

B. Read the lines from the story and answer the questions.

1. *'What did the king give you?'*
   a. Who said this and to whom?
   b. Why did the person go to the king?
   c. What did the king gift the person?
2. *'Where have you put the money?'*
   a. Who said this and to whom?
   b. Why did the speaker say so?
   c. What was the whole idea behind this plan?

Life Skills and Values

presence of mind

Think and answer.

1. What kind of a person was the barber? How was his personality different from that of his wife?
2. Do you think that the barber's wife was quick-witted? Why?
3. How did the barber's wife manage to scare the robbers away in the end?

Way with Words

Commonly Confused Words

In each sentence, underline the word that best fits the sentence. Then, make two sentences of your own using each word.

1. It's/Its mine!
2. How did you manage to lose/loose the money?
3. The library has been incredibly quiet/quite today.
4. It is there/their dog.
5. Whose/Who's party are you attending tomorrow?
6. Let's pray/prey for the victims of the accident.
7. Please buy paper and pens from the stationery/stationary shop.
8. With who/whom are you going to the party?

Grammar in Use

Demonstrative Pronouns and Interrogative Pronouns

Read this sentence.

This is their plot of land. **That** is their hut.

Here, **this** and **that** are demonstrative pronouns. *This* is used to refer to the plot of land, and *that* is used to refer to the hut.

Demonstrative pronouns take the place of specific persons, animals, places, things or ideas. **This, that, these** and **those** are demonstrative pronouns.

Example: **This** is the statue of Ashoka.

Interrogative pronouns are those that ask questions referring to a person, place or a thing. **Who, where, which** or **what** are interrogative pronouns.

Example: **Who** is the new barber in town?

A. Underline the pronouns in these sentences and state their types.

1. This is a book on rare plants.
2. Those are the new trees in the garden.
3. That is the car he wanted to buy.

4. Which was the right answer?
5. Where are the new socks?
6. These are the last few pieces left from the latest collection.
7. There are keys lying on the table. Whose is it?
8. This is the dress I was looking for.

Comparison of Adjectives

You have learned that adjectives have three degrees of comparison: **positive**, **comparative** and **superlative**.

We use the **comparative form** to compare people or things. We add **-er** after the adjective or we add **more** before the adjective to make the comparative form.

Examples: The barber's wife was **smarter** than the robbers.
It was **more pleasant** to sleep outdoors than in a room.

We use the **superlative form** to talk about the greatest degree of something. We add **-est** after the adjective or we add **most** before the adjective to make the superlative forms.

Examples: The barber was the **poorest** man in the city.
That was the **most difficult** exercise in the book.

B. Complete the sentences with the correct form of the adjectives.

1. Jupiter is the __________ planet in the solar system. (large)
2. This room is __________ than the other rooms in the house. (big)
3. I think learning French is __________ than learning German. (easy)
4. This treatment is __________ than the other treatment. (successful)
5. Cricket is the __________ sport in India. (popular)
6. Your sister is __________ than your brother. (friendly)
7. This is the __________ painting in the exhibition. (beautiful)
8. Today was the __________ day of the season. (hot)

Study Skills

Spell Check

Some words are misspelled frequently. For example, **magnificent** is often misspelled as **magnificient**.

Underline the correct spelling.

1. appropriate/apropriate/appropriet
2. maintenance/mentenance/maintainance
3. arguement/arrgument/argument
4. greatful/grateful/gratefull
5. ocassion/occasion/occassion
6. believe/belive/beleive
7. receive/recieve/receve
8. separet/separate/seperate
9. success/succes/succeess
10. ocurrence/occurrence/occurence

Listening and Speaking

A. You are going for a hike on a mountain trail. Listen to a set of instructions that will help you hike safely. Listen and number the sentences in the order you hear them.

- ☐ Stop and rest whenever you are tired.
- ☐ Carry a map and a compass and ensure you know how to use them.
- ☐ Maintain the correct posture while walking.
- ☐ Protect yourself from sunburn by wearing a hat and applying sunscreen lotion.
- ☐ Keep your eyes and mind on the trail while walking.
- ☐ Carry a torch and a whistle, which will help you in case you are lost.
- ☐ Use mosquito nets in your tent at night.
- ☐ You must hike at your own pace.
- ☐ Prevent and treat blisters at the earliest.
- ☐ Wear appropriate clothing depending upon the terrain and the weather.

B. Read the following sentences from the story.

Just as the robbers began waking up, she began ***howling*** *in a hollow voice. In the silence and darkness, the sound was terrifying.*

Here, the word *howling* has been used to express a feeling of fear and sorrow.

Listen to the sounds and mention what emotion each sound is expressing.

C. Do you think the story you read in this chapter is witty and humorous? Do you know similar stories? Narrate such a story in the class.

Pen it Down

21ST CENTURY Information Literacy

In the story, the robbers dug up the land and prepared it for planting seeds. Look at the pictures given on the next page. They depict the various stages of growing crops. Number them in the correct order.

Now, write answers to the following questions.

1. Who are the people in the pictures?
2. What are they doing?
3. What are the tractor and bullocks doing?
4. What do you think is being sprayed and why?
5. Why are food grains stored in granaries?

HC Contribution in others' lives

Self Assessment

Now I can

- read a story about how intelligence and wit can help us get out of difficult situations.
- identify commonly confused words and words that are often misspelled.
- use demonstrative and interrogative pronouns, and practise the comparison of adjectives.
- sequence sentences and pictures correctly, and answer questions based on pictures.

Read More

Indian Tales: This book by Romila Thapar is a collection of sixteen Indian tales told in a simple style for young readers. It has stories of gods and demons, of village folks and of animals.

Best Loved Folk Tales of India: This book by Pranab Chandra Roy Choudhury is a collection of some of the best stories from Indian mythology and folklore. It includes tales like 'The Clever Daughter-in-Law' and 'The Legend of Jayamala'.

9 Tintin in Tibet

graphic story

Hergé

Let's Get Started

Read the following infographic on Nepal and fill in the blanks. For the top five attractions, use the verbs from the help box to fill in the gaps.

NEPAL

TOP 5 ATTRACTIONS

1. ________ the UNESCO World Heritage sites in Kathmandu, Bhaktapur and Patan
2. ________ in the Everest, Annapurna and Langtang regions
3. ________ in scenic and peaceful Pokhara, the gateway to the Himalayas
4. ________ the rich wildlife of Nepal in Chitwan National Park
5. ________ to Lumbini, the birthplace of Gautam Buddha

relax	drive	trek
visit	observe	

THE EARTHQUAKE IN 2015

One of the most destructive ________ in the modern world took place on 25 April 2015 in Nepal, causing great damage to life and property. It recorded 7.8 on the Richter ________. Many temples were destroyed in Durbar Square and even the ________ in Kathmandu valley collapsed, where Christians used to pray regularly. Since ________ is already a poor country, the earthquake pushed it further into poverty.

MT EVEREST

Mt Everest is the ________ peak in the world at 8,848.86 metres. The China-Nepal border runs across its summit. The ________ people to climb it were Edmund Hillary and Tenzing Norgay. From Nepal, Kala Patthar, near Everest Base ________ is the ________ place to view Mt Everest.

Reading

The reporter, Tintin is on holiday in the Swiss Alps with his faithful dog, Snowy, and his close friends Captain Haddock – a retired sailor – and Professor Calculus, a half-deaf, absent-minded scientist. One day, Tintin begins to receive strange signs about a dear friend. Read on to find out more.

NEPAL AIR DISASTER
KATMANDU, Wednesday.—The D.C.3 missing since Monday on a flight from Patna to Katmandu is reported to have crashed in the Gosain Than massif.
It is believed that the aircraft, belonging to Indian Airways, was driven towards the Himalaya by a violent storm.
A search-plane yesterday spotted the wreckage of the aircraft in a remote and dangerous area. As soon as the news was received, a party of Sherpas set out for the peak where the aircraft crashed.
The aircraft is known to have carried 14 passengers and 4 crew.
BANDITS IN VIENNA RAID
Poor devils! What a dreadful place for a crash. They wouldn't stand a chance of surviving up there...
And that's what your beautiful mountains do for you!
DONG
The gong for dinner. Come on. I'm famished.
And after dinner...
Hmm! My queen's in danger. What shall I do? Protect her with my knight? No, that'd leave my bishop vulnerable. Suppose I advance that pawn?...
No, that won't work either... I shall have to do something else. Yes, my queen will have to fight a rearguard action... Right... then, with my next move I'll launch a flank attack with my other bishop... Then what will the enemy do? If he sees the danger, he'll cover his castle with a pawn...
In that case, I'll take the plunge and sacrifice my bishop. But he won't be sacrificed in vain! An eye for an eye: I shall take his castle... And there we are — check! Very neat! What do you say to that, eh Tintin?
CHANG!

Billions of blue blistering barnacles! You don't really have to sneeze like that, do you?
But... I... I... didn't sneeze.
I'm terribly sorry, I must have dropped off... I had a horrible nightmare...
A nightmare?
Yes. I was dreaming about Chang... you remember Chang, the boy I made friends with in China... I saw him... it was ghastly...
He was lying there hurt, half buried by snow... He was holding out his hands and calling to me, "Help, Tintin! help!" It was all so terribly real... I'm still quite stunned by it... Please do forgive me.
That's all right, don't worry. Forget it. You go on up to bed. You're dead tired.
I think you're right. Good night, Captain.
The next morning...
Hello there! Slept well?... No more dreams?
Good morning, Captain. No, no more dreams.
No dreams, but not much sleep, either. I was haunted by that picture of Chang lying in the snow, calling to me for help.
Rubbish! Dreams go by opposites, so they say. Don't think about it. Look, there's a letter for you, from Hong Kong.
Hong Kong?
Yes, look at the envelope. It's taken a long time to reach you. From Labrador Road to Marlinspike, then Nestor sent it on here.
Who's writing to me from Hong Kong?
BY AIR MAIL
PAR AVION
比國布魯塞尔
丁丁先生台啟
香港張仲文
Please forward:
Go Captain Haddock
Marlinspike Hall
Marlinspike
Mr. Tintin
Hotel des Sommets,
26, Labrador Road,
Vargèse
CHANG!

Honestly! Billions of blue bistering barnacles! You can't pretend this time that you've had another dream!
No, no! Look here: it really is a letter from Chang!
You must admit it's a remarkable coincidence. Yesterday evening I dreamt about him: this morning I get a letter from him. Extraordinary, isn't it?
Yes... I suppose so. What does he want, anyway?
Here, listen: "The brother of my most venerable adoptive father"... I didn't know that Mr. Wang Chen-Yee had a brother... "The brother of my most venerable adoptive father is living in London, where he has an antique shop. He has generously invited me to stay with him..." Hooray!
"Although unworthy of such an invitation I have accepted. Tomorrow I leave Hong Kong by air. I am filled with pleasure that I shall see your noble face once again". He's coming! Good!
Yes, fine... But, I say... this Chang, he's not like that little monster Abdullah, is he?
Chang? Why, Captain, he's one of the nicest people I know: quiet, unassuming - and with a heart of gold. You'll see!
Yes, and Chang's an old friend of yours too, isn't he, Snowy?
Professor Calculus! Wonderful news! Chang's coming! We're going to see CHANG again!
Champagne? At this hour!?
Chang's coming!... Tralala!
It is most reprehensible, Captain, to give this young man champagne, and in the morning too!
?
When's he coming, then... your... er... Son of Heaven?
Let's see.
He says: "I fly to Calcutta, then on to Nepal. My venerable adoptive father wishes me to visit Katmandu to pay my respects to his honourable cousin who has many children, and to take them presents."
Nepal?... Katmandu?... The plane that hit a mountain ... surely that was going to Katmandu?
Quick... this morning's paper. Perhaps there'll be some details of the crash.
Daily Reporter

coincidence: when two events happen at the same time without planning

glorious: wonderful

jagged: with sharp edges

fagged out: (informal use) very tired

air's like champagne: expression meaning that the air is clear, dry and pleasing

Alpine: related to the mountains, above a certain altitude

abolished: banned by law

massif: a group of mountains close to one another

remote: a place located far away from populated areas

wreckage: destroyed and broken pieces

raid: a surprise attack

famished: very hungry

vulnerable: open to being attacked by others

queen, knight, bishop, pawn, castle: chess pieces that move in specific ways during a game. The 'castle' is an old term, and it is called 'rook' now.

rearguard action, flank attack, check: different moves in chess

take the plunge: decide to so something risky

an eye for an eye: take revenge for something

haunted: (here) troubled by a memory of someone

barnacles: small sea creatures, with hard shells, that stick to rocks near the shore in large groups

ghastly: horrible

adoptive: related to someone through the legal act of adoption

stunned: shocked

antique: an object that is very old and valuable

venerable: respected

unassuming: quiet, not trying to appear important

reprehensible: behaviour or idea that is morally wrong

Literary term

hungry as a hunter: This is an example of a **simile**. Here the writer has compared the hunger felt by Tintin after his trek to that of a hunter who has returned after a long and hard day hunting for game.

Wordwise

The term **'Sherpa'** refers to a group of Himalayan people from Nepal or Tibet, often known for their mountaineering skills and knowledge of the area. They guided early Himalayan explorers, especially in Mount Everest expeditions.

Did You Know? G.K.

Nestor is Captain Haddock's faithful butler at his home in Marlinspike Hall in the English countryside.

Abdullah is a naughty Arab boy who appears in the *Tintin* comics, *Land of Black Gold* and in *The Red Sea Sharks*.

Professor Calculus' name refers to a branch of advanced mathematics, while **Captain Haddock's** name is taken from a fish popular in Scotland, his birthplace. Both names tell us about their professions – scientist and sailor.

About the author

Hergé (1907—1983) was the pen name of Belgian cartoonist Georges Prosper Remi. Born into a poor family, he began working as a cartoonist for newspapers and found success with the *Tintin* series. First published in 1929, *The Adventures of Tintin* series is one of the most popular comic series of all time. The books are loved for their detailed plots and real-life settings. Some of his other series are *Quick and Flupke* and *Jo, Zette and Jocko*. The graphic story you just read has been taken from one of his popular works, *Tintin in Tibet*.

Comprehension

Quick Recap

A. Answer these questions.

1. What does Tintin tell Captain Haddock towards the beginning of the comic?
2. What is Captain Haddock's response to this and why does he think so?
3. Who is referred to as 'Son of Heaven' in the comic? Which episode makes Tintin remember this person?
4. Give examples of onomatopoeia and alliteration from the comic.
5. What confusion does Professor Calculus suffer from? What was the actual situation?

B. Read the lines from the comic and answer the questions.

1. *'Poor devils! What a dreadful place for a crash.'*
   a. Who said these words?
   b. What crash is being referred to?
   c. How do we learn about this crash?
   d. Which other city is mentioned in the panel just before this?

2. *'Yes, look at the envelope. It's taken a long time to reach you.'*
   a. Who said these words and to whom?
   b. What were the speaker and the one being spoken to discussing?
   c. Who was the writer of the letter?
   d. From where was the letter written and where was it originally delivered? Why was it sent to the new location?

Life Skills and Values

interpreting clues

Think and answer.

1. From his presence throughout the extract and the various expressions that he displays, write a character sketch of the dog Snowy. Refer to panels **2** (page 1 row 1), **1** (page 2, row 3), **3** (page 3, row 2) and **3** (page 4, row 2) for help.
2. On the second page and the second row, there are three panels which look very similar to each other. Look closely and write a list of the similarities and differences between them.

21ST CENTURY Critical Thinking

Way with Words

PREFIX: *UN*

You know that a **prefix** is used before a word and helps to form new words with different meanings.

Example: Tintin felt **un**easy about his dream of Chang.

A. Complete the sentences using words formed by adding the prefix un- to the words in the box.

opposed	lock	happy	planned	decided	solved

1. The boy cannot find his cricket bat; so he is very ____________.
2. Please ____________ the door with this key.
3. He is still ____________ as to whether he should contest the elections.
4. He won the contest ____________.
5. Please practise for the test with this ____________ question paper.
6. He went on an ____________ trip.

PHRASAL VERBS WITH *RUN*

A **phrasal verb** includes a verb and another element, such as an adverb or a preposition.

Example: Professor Calculus **ran into** Tintin and Snowy on his way to breakfast at the hotel.
(run into = meet someone unexpectedly)

B. Find out the meanings of the following phrasal verbs.

1. run around 2. run away 3. run for 4. run into 5. run on

C. Complete the sentences using the phrasal verbs from exercise B. You may have to make some necessary changes.

1. Electric cars ____________ electricity and not petrol.
2. Shanaya is ____________ the post of School Captain.
3. He suddenly ____________ his English teacher after twenty years.
4. I used to ____________ this area when I was a small boy.
5. We must not ____________ from our responsibilities.

Grammar in Use

CONDITIONAL SENTENCES WITH 'IF'

Look at the sentence.

Tintin realised that **if** he wanted to save his friend, he had to act immediately.

Here, **if** is the word used to state the condition that he has to 'act immediately' in order to 'save his friend'.

A. Complete these conditional sentences.

1. I think you will fail if ____________
2. If you run so fast ____________
3. Don't worry. If you plan ahead ____________
4. We can still reach in time if ____________
5. If you want to buy the latest clothes ____________
6. Rahul will have to renew his passport if ____________

COORDINATING CONJUNCTIONS

Coordinating conjunctions connect phrases, clauses and sentences.

There are seven coordinating conjunctions. They are given in this table.

Conjunction	Purpose
for	suggests a purpose or a reason for something **Example:** I am so tired **for** I have been trekking since morning.
and	joins similar statements or thoughts **Example:** In that case, I'll take the plunge **and** sacrifice my bishop.

nor	suggests a second negative idea **Example:** Captain Haddock didn't like the mountains, **nor** did he understand Tintin's love for them.
but	joins two ideas or sentences that are the opposite of each other **Example:** **But** if this goes on, I'll have no paws left!
or	shows a choice between two things or ideas **Example:** Chang may leave for Kathmandu today **or** tomorrow.
yet	introduces an idea which is surprising because it is different from a previous fact that has just been mentioned **Example:** Snowy was tired, **yet** he did not leave his master's side.
so	shows result or effect **Example:** Tintin was very tired, **so** he went to bed.

B. Join the sentences using suitable coordinating conjunctions. You may have to make some changes.

1. They were rich. They were miserly.
2. I overslept. I missed the school bus.
3. That shirt cannot be mine. It is too big to fit me.
4. He had never been to school. He wrote an award-winning book.
5. He is not rich. He is not hardworking.
6. The team tried hard. The team did not win the match.
7. We are worried about our dog's health. She is very old.

C. Complete the sentences using appropriate coordinating conjunctions from the brackets.

1. Usually, I like to run __________ today I am walking. (yet/but)
2. It is raining heavily, __________ you must wear your raincoat. (and/so)
3. The old man is always crying, __________ he is very lonely. (for/but)
4. I don't like butter __________ cheese. (or/nor)
5. Mala __________ her family friends are going for a picnic. (and/or)
6. Manoj ran fast, __________ he did not win the race. (and/yet)
7. Ram loves to act in plays __________ he is very good at acting. (for/and)
8. She refuses to meet me, __________ will she talk to me on the phone. (for/nor)

Study Skills

Pronounce Well

Words with Silent Letters

In the word 'island', the letter **'s'** is not pronounced.

Answer the following questions.

1. Which word has silent **k**?
   a. kite b. know c. king
2. Which word has silent **t**?
   a. tiger b. felt c. listen
3. Which word has silent **h**?
   a. hour b. hill c. hero
4. Which word has silent **g**?
   a. game b. design c. great
5. Which word has silent **b**?
   a. boy b. bulb c. debt

Listening and Speaking

In pairs, do the following role-playing activity.

Refer to panel 1, page 2, row 3. Imagine that you are Tintin and are embarrassed by your actions. Apologize to the other hotel guests in the activity room for the distress you caused them. One of you can play the role of Tintin and the other can play the role of one of the guests. Use polite language to convey your sincerest apologies to the guest. The guest can then respond appropriately. Use these words and phrases as well the following example to guide you.

Example: **Hotel staff:** My apologies, Captain Haddock. I shouldn't have rung the dinner bell so loudly.
Captain Haddock: That's alright. No harm done, but you did startle me.
Hotel staff: I am so sorry, once again. I hope I didn't cause you too much distress. I shall be careful from next time.
Captain Haddock: Thank you. I appreciate it.

Useful words and phrases:

- Sorry!
- I shall be careful in future.
- Please accept my sincerest apologies.
- Thank you so much for understanding.
- Oops!
- I am sorry.
- It was my fault.
- How can I make up for it?

Pen it Down

Write an informal letter as Tintin thanking Chang for his letter and sharing your happiness on his upcoming visit as well as concern for his well-being.

The following points can be included in your letter:

- address of the letter writer and recipient as well as date
- how you felt upon receiving the letter
- what you are looking forward to after learning about the information shared in the letter
- the reason for the delay in responding to the letter
- where you are currently located and what you are doing there
- your concern about the crash

HC Contributions in relationships (friends)

Self Assessment

Now I can

- read a graphic story about a boy reporter and his friends.
- use phrasal verbs with *run* and practise using prefixes with *-un*.
- use coordinating conjunctions and make conditional sentences using *if*.
- make an apology and write an informal letter.

Read More

The Red Sea Sharks: This comic by Hergé narrates Tintin, Snowy and Captain Haddock's travels in the fictional West Asian country of Khemed. There they help the ruler, Emir Ben Kalish Ezab, to regain control over the country from dangerous enemies, such as Roberto Rastapopoulos.

Asterix and the Golden Sickle: This comic by René Goscinny (text) and Albert Uderzo (art) is about Asterix and Obelix's adventurous trip to Lutetia to buy a replacement golden sickle for Getafix.

light verse

10
Sick

Healthy Living

Shel Silverstein

SUSTAINABLE DEVELOPMENT GOALS
3 GOOD HEALTH AND WELL-BEING

Let's Get Started

The United Nations Sustainable Development Goal 3 is about good health and well-being. It states that everyone should have access to basic healthcare and be able to lead a healthy lifestyle.

Read the questions and tick the answers that you think promotes healthy food habits.

1. What is the main problem with junk food?
   - It is not good to taste. ☐
   - It contains too much sugar or salt. ☐
   - It is packaged attractively. ☐
2. Which foods do we need to eat every day?
   - a lot of rice, chapati or some other cereal ☐
   - some items from all food groups ☐
   - any food that appeals to our taste ☐
3. Why should we eat small meals across the day?
   - because eating is a fun activity ☐
   - because this promotes healthy digestion ☐
   - because eating is better than exercising ☐

HC **Learning and Awareness:** Separate needs of self and body

Reading

What do you do when you are sick? Read this poem about a girl pretending to be sick.

'I cannot go to school today,'
Said little Peggy Ann McKay.

'I have the **measles** and the **mumps**,
A gash, a rash and purple bumps.

My mouth is wet, my throat is dry,
I'm going blind in my right eye.

My tonsils are as big as rocks,
I've counted sixteen chicken pox
And there's one more—that's seventeen,
And don't you think my face looks green?
My leg is cut—my eyes are blue—
It might be instamatic flu.

I cough and sneeze and gasp and choke,
I'm sure that my left leg is broke—
My hip hurts when I move my chin,
My belly button's caving in,
My back is **wrenched**, my ankle's **sprained**,
My '**pendix** pains each time it rains.[1]

My nose is cold, my toes are **numb**.
I have a **sliver** in my thumb.

My neck is stiff, my voice is weak,
I hardly whisper when I speak.

My tongue is filling up my mouth,
I think my hair is falling out.

My elbow's bent, my spine ain't straight,
My temperature is one-o-eight.

My brain is shrunk, I cannot hear,
There is a hole inside my ear.

I have a **hangnail**, and my heart is—what?
What's that? What's that you say?
You say today is … Saturday?
G'bye, I'm going out to play!'

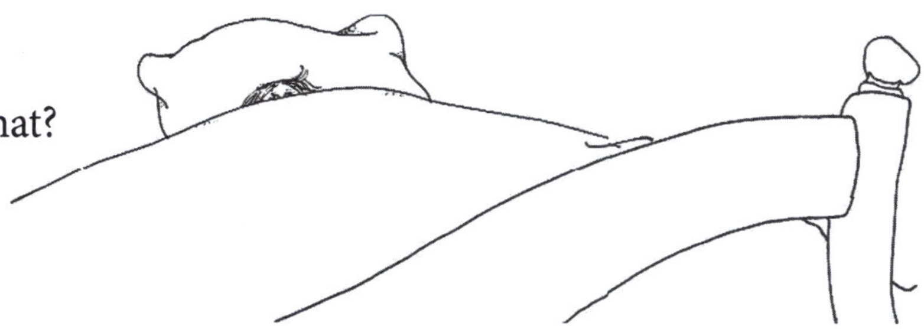

measles: an illness that produes red spots on the skin

mumps: a disease that causes a painful swelling of the neck

wrenched: (here) injured because of sudden movement

sprained: injured by a sudden and violent twist

'pendix: shortened form for appendix, a small closed tube inside the body, which is attached to our digestive system

numb: without any feeling

sliver: (here) a small thin piece of wood or metal

hangnail: a loose piece of skin near the bottom of your fingernail

Literary term

1. This line and the preceding four lines are examples of **hyperbole**. The girl uses exaggeration to make the listener believe she is very ill.

About the poet

Shel Silverstein (1930–1999) was an American poet who became famous for his books for children. *The Giving Tree* and the poem 'Where the Sidewalk Ends' are some of his noted works.

Comprehension

Quick Recap

A. Answer the questions.

1. Why was Peggy feeling sick?
2. How many chicken pox did she have?
3. What had happened to her legs and eyes?
4. Find three examples of alliteration from the poem.
5. What did Peggy mean by the term 'instamatic flu'? What do you think is the characteristic feature of 'instamatic flu'?

B. Read the lines and answer the questions.

1. *'My tonsils are as big as rocks.*

   I have counted sixteen chicken pox'

   a. Identify the figure of speech in this extract.

   b. What does the speaker mean by counting chicken pox?

   c. What happened immediately after the speaker counted the number of chicken poxes she had?

2. *'You say today is ... Saturday?*

   G'bye, I'm going out to play!'

   a. Why was the girl so startled to hear that it was Saturday?

   b. Why did she go out to play?

   c. What cured the little girl of her illnesses?

Life Skills and Values being honest, admitting mistakes

Think and answer.

1. Peggy Ann McKay was not sick. She was just making excuses to avoid going to school. Do you think she was wrong in making these excuses?
2. What adjective can be used to describe Peggy Ann McKay? Give examples from the poem to support your answer.

Way with Words

Different Types of Doctors

Doctors often specialise in treating a particular type of disease.

A. Match the following doctors with their specializations.

A	B
1. cardiologist	a. treats brain and nervous system-related problems
2. paediatrician	b. treats eye-related problems
3. ophthalmologist	c. treats skin-related problems
4. dermatologist	d. treats children of age one day to 16 years
5. orthopaedic	e. treats heart-related problems
6. neurologist	f. treats bone-related problems

Similes

Read this sentence.

My tonsils are as big as rocks.

This is an example of a **simile**, where a similarity is drawn between two dissimilar things. The words 'as' and 'like' are usually used in similes for the comparisons.

B. Complete these similes using appropriate words.

1. as free as ____________
2. as heavy as ____________
3. as quick as ____________
4. as steady as ____________
5. as tall as ____________
6. as white as ____________
7. as brave as ____________
8. as blind as ____________

Grammar in Use

Determiners: Many, Much, Most, Some, Any

Many, much, most, some, any are words placed in front of nouns to specify quantity or number.

Many and **much** express a large quantity.

Examples: There are **many** science students in the class.
He doesn't have **much** money.

We use **most** for quantities, amounts and degree.

Example: She exercises on **most** mornings.

We do not normally use **some** in negative and interrogative sentences. We use **any** in such sentences.

Examples: Did you see **any** elephants?
We don't have **any** pets.
We saw **some** lions, but didn't see **any** tigers in the wildlife reserve.
Would you like **some** coffee?

A. Fill the blanks with the correct determiners.

1. We need ____________ (any/some) more food on the table.
2. ____________ (Most/Much) desserts are sweet.
3. May I have ____________ (some/any) sugar in my tea, please?
4. There isn't ____________ (some/any) cold water in the kitchen.
5. I don't agree with ____________ (much/many) of what you said.
6. Are there ____________ (much/any) parcels for me?
7. I am so thirsty. Can I have ____________ (many/some) water, please?
8. We have ____________ (many/any) trees in front of our house.
9. How ____________ (most/many) times have I told you to tell the truth?
10. ____________ (Most/Some) of India gets rain in the months of July and August.

Future Continuous Tense

Read this sentence.

Tintin **will be spending** some time in Nepal.

The highlighted words tell us that the action will continue to happen in the future.

The **future continuous tense** indicates an ongoing action that will take place in the future.

B. Fill in the blanks with the future continuous tense by using the verbs in brackets.

1. Babu ____________ his best friend after the pandemic is over. (meet)
2. The flight ____________ at 9 p.m. (arrive)
3. I ____________ an article on good health tomorrow. (write)
4. Samaira ____________ in a hotel near the beach. (stay)
5. When mother comes home, I ____________ yoga. (do)
6. Heena ____________ her grandmother in the morning. (call)

Irregular Verbs

Verbs can be divided into two categories: **regular** and **irregular verbs**. We can form the past tense of irregular verbs by changing the vowel in the base form.

Examples: break → broke   draw → drew   eat → ate

C. Fill in the blanks with the simple past tense of the given verbs.

1. The glass ____________ (fall) from the shelf and ____________ (break).
2. My sister ____________ (draw) a beautiful picture.
3. I ____________ (eat) at an Italian restaurant yesterday.
4. Ramit ____________ (forget) to bring his lunch.
5. I ____________ (grow) up in a small town near London.
6. They ____________ (sing) cheerfully in the choir.
7. Sheena ____________ (wear) a beautiful dress last night.
8. The ship ____________ (sink) after colliding with an iceberg.

Study Skills

Pronounce Well

Read the words in the box aloud and notice the difference in the sounds of the highlighted vowel. Place them in the two columns according to the sound of i.

tonsils	isle	whines	in	mile
wide	inside	filling	ignoring	dying

'i' as in island	'i' as in sick

Listening and Speaking

Listen to an extract from the poem 'Peanut Butter Sandwich' by Shel Silverstein. Then, mark the following statements as true (T) or false (F).

1. This poem is about a wise old king.
2. The king's clothes were new and shining.
3. Children were only taught how to make peanut butter in school.
4. The king loved to eat cake and drink soup.
5. The king laughed after having his peanut butter sandwich.
6. The king's mother thought he had committed suicide.

Pen it Down

Write a few sentences describing an imaginary ailment that prevents you from going to school. No names should be written on the paper. Collect the papers and then randomly redistribute. Read out what is written on the paper. The class can vote for the best imaginary ailment!

Self Assessment

Now I can

- read about the excuses children make when they do not want to go to school.
- match doctors with their medical specilizations and practise similes.
- use the future continuous tense, determiners and practise irregular verbs.
- pronounce words with *i* correctly and write about an imaginary ailment.

Read More

Ickle Me, Pickle Me, Tickle Me Too: This poem by Shel Silverstein is about Ickle Me, Pickle Me and Tickle Me Too. It narrates how the three of them went on an adventure ride and what befalls them.

The Unicorn: This poem, also by Shel Silverstein, is a part of his collection of poetry for children, *Where the Sidewalk Ends*. It talks about why there are no unicorns in our world.

Suspense and Mystery

11

The Incident of the Letter

Robert Louis Stevenson

Let's Get Started

Test your detective skills by using the secret code given below. Use the clues in brackets to fill in the terms related to mysteries.

For example: If the letter in the clue is an A, fill in the blank with a z. The words in the help words will guide you.

secret code: A=z B=y C=x D=w E=v F=u G=t H=s I=r J=q K=p L=o M=n N=m O=l P=k Q=j R=i S=h T=g U=f V=e W=d X=c Y=b Z=a

suspect plot detective crime witness mystery alibi motive

1. the sequence of events in a story (KOLG) ______
2. an act that breaks the law (XIRNV) ______
3. someone who observes a crime being committed (DRGMVHH) ______
4. a person who might have committed a crime (HFHKVXG) ______
5. the main reason due to which a crime is committed (NLGREV) ______
6. something that is secret or unknown (NBHGVIB) ______
7. a person who uses clues and solves crimes (WVGVXGREV) ______
8. the excuse given to show that someone was elsewhere when the crime was committed (ZORYR) ______

HC **Feelings:** Contributions in societal relationships

Reading

This is an extract from the novel* Dr Jekyll and Mr Hyde. *A murder has taken place. The suspect is Mr Hyde and the victim is Sir Danvers Carew, a Member of Parliament and one of Mr Utterson's clients. Mr Utterson leads the police to Hyde's residence, only to find him missing. Find out what happens next.

It was late in the afternoon when Mr Utterson reached Dr Jekyll's door and was shown inside by Poole. He was led to the laboratory. It was the first time that he had visited his friend's quarters and he eyed the dimly lit room with curiosity and distaste. He crossed the **theatre**, once crowded with eager students and now lying silent, the tables topped with chemical apparatus, crates and packing straw scattered on the floor and the light falling dimly through the fog. It was a large, business-like room with iron-barred windows that faced the court. A fire burned in the **grate**; a white lamp was lighted on the chimney-shelf for better lighting; and there sat Dr Jekyll, near the fire, looking deadly sick. Without rising to meet him, he held out a cold hand and welcomed him in a changed voice.

theatre: (here) a room where surgeries are performed

grate: a framework of metal bars in a fireplace

shuddered: trembled suddenly and violently, as if from horror and fear

feverish: nervous

'And now,' said Mr Utterson, as soon as Poole had left them, 'you have heard the news?'

The doctor **shuddered.** 'They were crying it in the square,' he said. 'I heard them in my dining room.'

'One word,' said the lawyer. 'Carew was my client, but so are you and I want to know what I am doing. You have not been mad enough to hide this fellow?'

'Utterson,' cried the doctor, 'I swear to God I will never set eyes on him again. He is quite safe, mark my words, and he will never be heard of again.'

The lawyer did not like his friend's **feverish** manner. 'You seem pretty sure of him,' he said, 'and for your sake, I hope you are right. If it came to a trial, your name might appear.'

'I have grounds for certainty that I cannot share with anyone,' replied Jekyll. 'But there is one thing on which you may advise me. I have received a letter and

I wonder whether I should show it to the police. I should like to leave it in your hands, Utterson. I trust you completely.'

'You fear, I suppose, that it might lead to Hyde's detection?' asked the lawyer.

'No,' said the other. 'I hardly care what happens to Hyde. I was thinking of my own reputation, which this hateful business had rather damaged.'

Utterson thought for a while. He was surprised at his friend's selfishness and yet relieved by it. 'Well,' he said at last, 'let me see the letter.'

The letter, written in an odd, upright handwriting and signed 'Edward Hyde', stated that Dr Jekyll, whom the writer had long unworthily repaid for a thousand generosities, need not be alarmed for his safety as he had a sure means of escape. The lawyer liked this letter well enough and he blamed himself for suspecting any friendship between Mr Hyde and Dr Jekyll.

'Do you have the envelope?' he asked.

'I burned it,' replied Jekyll, 'before I realised what I was doing. But it had no postmark. The note was delivered by hand.'

'Shall I keep this and **sleep upon it**?' asked Utterson.

'I want you to judge for me entirely, as I have lost all confidence in myself,' was the reply.

'Well, I shall consider,' returned the lawyer. 'And now one word more; was it Hyde who dictated the terms in your will about that disappearance?'

The doctor felt faint but shut his mouth tight and nodded.

'I knew it,' said Utterson. 'He meant to murder you. You have had a fine escape.'

'I have had a lesson,' returned the doctor solemnly.

Did You Know? G.K.

The book *Dr Jekyll and Mr Hyde* was written by R. L. Stevenson in less than a week. He took three days to write the first draft and another three days to write the final draft.

sleep upon it: think about something before taking a decision

circulars: letters or advertisements distributed to a large number of people

sullied: damaged

critic: a person who is qualified to make judgments about the qualities of something

'Oh God, Utterson, what a lesson I have had![1]' And he covered his face for a moment with his hands.

On his way out, the lawyer stopped and asked Poole, 'A letter was handed in today. What was the messenger like?'

But Poole was sure that nothing had come except by post, and that too, only **circulars.** The lawyer left with his fears renewed. In the streets, the newsboys were shouting hoarsely, 'Special edition. Shocking murder of an MP!' That was the end of one friend and client, and he was afraid that another's name would be **sullied.**

After a while, he sat on one side of his own fireplace, while Mr Guest, his head clerk, sat on the other side. The fog still lay thick outside while the lamps shone dimly and the sounds of the city were faint. But the room was gay with firelight. There were very few secrets that he kept from Mr Guest. The clerk had often visited the doctor on business, he knew Poole; no doubt he had heard of Mr Hyde's frequent visits to the house. Above all, he was an expert **critic** of handwriting. The clerk would hardly read so strange a document without dropping a remark, and by that remark, Mr Utterson might decide his future course of action.

'This is a sad business about Sir Danvers,' he said.

'Yes, sir, indeed. The public is very upset about it,' said Guest. 'The man, of course, was mad.'

'I should like to hear your views on that,' replied Utterson. 'I have a document here in his handwriting; it is between ourselves, for it is an ugly business. But there it is, a murderer's autograph.'

Literary term

1. This is an example of **repetition.** The phrase 'have had a lesson' is repeated to emphasise Dr Jekyll's regret for trusting Mr Hyde.

Guest's eyes brightened and he studied it eagerly. 'No, sir,' he said, 'not mad, but it is an odd hand.' Just then, the servant entered with a note.

'Is that from Dr Jekyll, sir?' inquired the clerk. 'I thought I knew the writing. Anything private, Mr Utterson?'

> quaint: odd
>
> forges: produces a false copy illegally

'Only an invitation to dinner. Why? Do you want to see it?'

'One moment. I thank you, sir,' said the clerk as he held the two sheets of paper alongside and compared their contents. 'Thank you, sir,' he said at last, returning both. 'It is a very interesting signature.'

There was a pause, then Mr Utterson asked uneasily, 'Why did you compare them, Guest?'

'Well, sir,' returned the clerk, 'there is a rather strange resemblance; the two hands are in many points identical, only differently sloped.'

'Rather **quaint**,' said Utterson.

'It is, as you say, rather quaint,' returned Guest.

'I wouldn't speak of this note, you know,' said the master.

'No, sir,' said the clerk. 'I understand.'

Wordwise

The word 'critic' comes from the Latin word *criticus*, which means able to judge.

But as soon as Mr Utterson was alone that night, he locked the note into his safe, where it lay from that time onwards. 'What!' he thought. 'Henry Jekyll **forges** for a murderer!' And his blood ran cold in his veins.

About the author

Robert Louis Balfour Stevenson (1850–1894) was a Scottish novelist, poet, essayist and travel writer. *An Inland Voyage*, was his first book. His most famous novel is *The Treasure Island*.

Comprehension

Quick Recap

A. Answer the questions in a few lines.

1. What kind of a person was Dr Jekyll?
2. What kind of a relationship did Dr Jekyll and Mr Utterson share?

3. What did Dr Jekyll tell Mr Utterson about the letter? Was Dr Jekyll being truthful?
4. What was Mr Guest's analysis of the two sets of handwriting that he compared?
5. What was Dr Jekyll's motive for showing the letter to Mr Utterson?

B. Read the lines from the passage and answer the questions.

1. *'You have heard the news.'*
   a. Who said this and to whom?
   b. What was the speaker referring to?
   c. Why did the speaker visit the other person's house?
2. *'Yes sir, indeed. The public is very upset about it.'*
   a. Who said this and to whom?
   b. What was the public so upset about?
   c. What was the speaker asked to do next?

Life Skills and Values — being analytical

Think and answer.

1. Do you think Dr Jekyll and Mr Hyde could have been a single person instead of being two different people?
2. Why do you think Dr Jekyll lied about the letter?
3. What was so startling about the similarity between the two sets of handwriting?

Way with Words

ANALOGIES

Read this comparison.

Laboratory is to chemical apparatus as envelope is to letter.

In the above statement, we are comparing the relationship between two pairs of things. This type of comparison is called an **analogy**.

Identify the correct option for each analogy.

1. **rose: flower**
   spade: ______________ a. instrument b. tool c. garden
2. **singer: concert**
   clown: ______________ a. office b. factory c. circus

3. **dentist: teeth**

barber: __________ a. hair b. nose c. head

4. **pack: suitcase**

wrap: __________ a. computer b. gift c. hammer

Grammar in Use

Present Perfect Tense

Read these sentences.

I **have received** a letter.

He **has done** a horrible crime.

You **have had** a narrow escape.

The words in bold indicate the present perfect tense.

The **present perfect tense** refers to an action or state that either occurred at an indefinite time in the past, or began in the past and continued to the present time.

The present perfect tense is formed by using **have/has** + the past participle.
We use **has** with singular subjects and **have** with plural subjects.

A. Fill in the blanks with the present perfect tense by using the verbs in brackets.

1. She __________ her project. (submit)
2. I __________ that he is not well. (hear)
3. My driver __________ a free trip to Kashmir. (win)
4. I __________ the Russian ballet that is in town right now. (see)
5. You __________ me in difficult situations. (always help)
6. Mehraab __________ at last in climbing Mount Everest. (succeed)
7. Ria __________ to join a computer course. (decide)
8. I __________ the essay myself. (write)

Past Perfect Tense

Read these sentences.

When we arrived, the train **had left**.

If I **had woken up** earlier, I would have caught my school bus.

The words in bold indicate the past perfect tense.

The **past perfect tense** is used to talk about actions that were completed before some point in the past.

The past perfect tense is formed by using **had** + past participle.

B. Fill in the blanks with the past perfect tense by using the verbs in brackets.

1. I ____________ to London before we went there last year. (never be)
2. It ____________ raining when I bought an umbrella. (already stop)
3. When I ____________ home yesterday, my mother had already left for the market. (reach)
4. My sister ____________ a lot of chocolate by the time lunch was served. (eat)
5. My father did not have any money because he ____________ his wallet in the metro. (lose)
6. He kept falling ill because he ____________ exercising. (stop)

Study Skills

Pronounce Well

PRONUNCIATION OF WORDS WITH THE LETTER 's'

The letter **s** can be pronounced in three different ways. It can sound like 's' as in **s**un, mou**s**e, dre**ss**; 'z' as in i**s**, wa**s**, plea**s**e; and 'sh' as in ten**s**ion, **s**ure.

Read out the words given in the box and categorise them according to the sound of s.

sand	salt	stall	rest	saw	toes	trees
years	cows	smell	snack	sugar	ensure	stick

Listening and Speaking

Listen to a short story and answer the questions.

1. What question did the Professor ask while holding the glass in his hand?
2. What was his answer to this question?
3. What would happen if he held the glass for a day?
4. What do you think caused the ache in the arm?
5. What do you learn from this story?

Pen it Down

A. Write a letter to the Police Commissioner of your city, informing him about the poor condition of law and order in your locality.

You may include the following points:

- the alarming rise in robberies and crimes in your area
- how it has become unsafe to walk in the locality and play in the parks
- inaction of the local police station despite informing them of the situation

B. In the story, Mr Utterson received an invitation from Dr Jekyll. Read the sample message from the doctor, inviting the lawyer for dinner.

Now, write a message accepting or declining Dr Jekyll's invitation.

Remember to include the following:

- name of the receiver
- reasons for accepting or declining the invitation
- name of the sender at the bottom
- date at the time of writing

19 December 1885

Dear Utterson,

As you are aware, this dreadful affair has had quite an impact on my nerves.

To take my mind off the unfortunate event, I have organised a small dinner party at my house tomorrow night at 8 p.m.

I will look forward to your delightful company.

Yours sincerely,

Henry Jekyll

Self Assessment

Now I can

- observe details about characters, settings and events in a story.
- understand analogies and practise using the present and past perfect tenses.
- identify different pronunciations of the letter **s**, and write a formal letter and a message.

Read More

The Merry Men: This short story by Robert Louis Stevenson is set on a fictional island. The people there loot ships that have wrecked on the island's shore.

The Black Arrow: A Tale of the Two Roses: This adventure novel by R. L. Stevenson is set in the time of King Henry VI. It is about a group called The Black Arrow and their adventures.

12

Ambition

Be Careful What You Wish For

Arden Davidson

Let's Get Started

What do you want to be when you grow up? Complete this manifesto about what you wish to do in life and how you want to go about achieving your goal. Also, think and write how you might help others while fulfilling your wish.

Name: ______________________________

Your wish in life: ______________________________

Steps to achieve this goal:

____

____

____

One way you might help others:

____

____

Learning and Awareness: Difference between knowing and assuming

Reading

Have you ever wished for something and then regretted that wish? In the poem, Arnie,

the apple, is wishing for something. Find out if his wish does come true.

Arnie the apple hung from a tree
in an orchard a mile wide.
And every day the **pickers** would come
and **haul** dozens of apples inside.

They'd pick the prettiest of the bunch,
filling their baskets and pails.
But they always passed by Arnie,
ignoring his **whines and wails**[1].

'Please pick me!', Arnie would cry
each time the pickers **sauntered** by.
'I want to go inside with you!',
cried Arnie till he turned bright blue.

But the pickers ignored him day after day,
while Arnie hung there in **dismay**,
trying to nurse his **shattered** pride,
dying to be picked, to be taken inside.

Each new dawn he'd do a trick
like spinning around on his twig.
But the **picky** pickers never stopped
for apples that weren't big.

Or juicy or red or bright or sweet.
Poor Arnie was none of these things.
He wasn't completely quite full grown
and he had some **nicks and dings**.

He dreamed what it was like inside;
lights and music all around.
Arnie just wanted to go there so badly
he flung himself to the ground.

The next day the pickers came along
and saw him lying there.
They took him inside and Arnie thought,
'This is it! I'm finally there!'

But when Arnie the Apple looked around
he realised his dreams were false,
cause in less than fifteen minutes
he was Arnie Applesauce.

pickers: (here) people who pick fruits for money

haul: carry off something with a lot of effort

whines and wails: noises of pain and sadness

sauntered: walked in a slow and relaxed way

dismay: strong feeling of sadness

shattered: greatly damaged

picky: choosy

nicks and dings: cuts and dents

Literary term

1. This is an example of **alliteration**. The consonant sound 'w' has been repeated in closely placed words.

About the poet

Arden Davidson is an American poet best known for her book *Playing Hopscotch on a Rubber Roof*. It is a collection of poems for children and was published in 2006.

Comprehension

Quick Recap

A. Answer the questions in a few lines.

1. Who is the poet talking about in the poem?
2. What was the wish of the one being spoken about?
3. What does the poet mean by 'each new dawn'?
4. What do you think the 'inside', where the apples were taken, actually is?
5. Why did the pickers ignore the one being spoken about and not take him inside initially?

B. Choose the correct answers.

1. Where was the tree from which Arnie hung?
   a. in a forest b. in a park c. in an orchard
2. What did Arnie do when he saw the pickers?
   a. laughed b. cried in grief c. fell on the pickers
3. How did the pickers move in the orchard?
   a. in a slow and relaxed manner b. in a great hurry c. at a normal pace
4. What did Arnie do one day in frustration?
   a. twisted and turned b. talked to the pickers c. fell to the ground
5. Arnie's dreams were
   a. shattered. b. fulfilled. c. non-existent.

Life Skills and Values logical reasoning

Think and answer.

1. Did Arnie like what happened to him in the end? Give reasons for your answer.
2. How is the title of the poem relevant to its message? Give examples from the poem to support your answer.

Way with Words

A. Match the words to their meanings.

Meaning	Word
1. a narrow way	a. passport
2. an official document issued by the foreign office of a government which identifies one as a citizen of a country and allows one to travel abroad	b. password
3. a book that keeps record of bank transactions	c. passage
4. a person who is travelling in a vehicle	d. passive
5. a secret word used to gain access	e. passbook
6. not active or not participating	f. passenger

B. Make sentences with any five words from exercise A.

Grammar in Use

Direct and Indirect Speech

There are two ways of reporting what a person says: in **direct speech** and in **indirect speech**.

Direct speech is repeating the exact words as spoken by the speaker.

Example: Arnie thought, 'This is it! I'm finally there!'

In direct speech:

- The exact words of the speaker are put within inverted commas ('…').
- There is a comma after the reporting verb and before the quote begins.
- The first word inside the inverted commas starts with a capital letter.

Indirect speech is reporting what a speaker said without quoting his/her exact words.

Example: Arnie thought with relief that he was finally there.

In indirect speech:

- The inverted commas as well as the comma after the reporting verb are removed.
- The conjunction **that** introduces the words spoken by the speaker.
- The tense of the verb usually changes.
- If the reporting verb is in the present or future tense, the tense of the verb is not changed at all. But, if the reporting verb is in the past tense, the tense is changed to a corresponding form of the past tense.
- The first and second person pronouns (**I**, **you**) and possessive adjectives (**my**, **your**) are changed to the person of the subject of the reporting verb.

A. Change the following sentences into indirect speech.

1. The teacher said, 'If you work hard, you will pass.'
2. Ravi said, 'I must go as soon as possible.'
3. Mala said, 'Let's wait for her to come back.'
4. Pooja asked Chirag, 'Are you going on the school trip?'
5. Parul said, 'Father, I want a new bicycle.'
6. The principal said, 'Tomorrow will be a holiday.'
7. The workers said, 'Please buy us better tools to do the job properly.'

B. Change the following sentences into direct speech.

1. The teacher told Akash that he was not doing his work neatly.
2. He asked me if I had brought his notes.
3. The judge told the lawyer to speak to the point.
4. My mother requested me not to go out in the rain.
5. The servant begged his master to forgive him.
6. Our coach told us that the match was on the next day.
7. Sheeba asked me if I could buy a new dress for her.

Study Skills

Use Your Dictionary

PHRASAL VERBS WITH 'OFF'

Use your dictionary to find the meanings of these phrasal verbs with off and use them to complete these sentences. You may have to change the tense of the verb.

let off set off rub off put off call off see off take off

1. The confidence of the captain __________ on the team.

2. He went to __________ his parents at the station.
3. I was __________ by the behaviour of the hosts at the party.
4. After preparing for months, they __________ for the trip.
5. The student was __________ by the principal quite easily.
6. It was so hot that I had to __________ my sweater.
7. The match was __________ because of bad weather.

Listening and Speaking

Say these words aloud. Identify the alliterative words in each set.

1. bear	bunnies	rabbit	big	sheep
2. wild	rain	west	wish	wind
3. time	shell	sea	home	she
4. dart	bark	dim	car	dog
5. ant	music	mike	mud	much

Pen it Down

21st Century Productivity

You read a poem about Arnie's wish. Now, write a short poem about any one of your wishes. Why do you wish for that thing and how will you feel if that wish is fulfilled? Use as many rhyming words as you can.

Self Assessment

Now I can

- read a poem on wish fulfilment and relate it to real-life situations.
- use direct and indirect speech and write a short poem.
- understand the idiomatic usage of phrasal verbs with *off*.

Read More

George, Who Played with a Dangerous Toy: This poem by Hilaire Belloc is about a little boy who was given a huge balloon. The balloon caught fire and caused an accident.

Puppy and I: This poem by A. A. Milne is about a small boy looking for a friend to play with him. Everyone he meets on the way is busy, except for a puppy.

Be Creative!

A. In 'Tintin in Tibet', you learn about Chang who wants to visit London from Hong Kong. Divide the class into five groups. One student in the group will choose a country that he/she would like to go to. The other members of the group will take turns to guess the country. After one person takes a guess, the student who chose the country must give a hint in relation to the country they have chosen. Each hint can be used only once.

B. The **main idea** is the most important idea in a story. The **details** in the story give more information about the main idea.

Read the passage. Then, choose the correct answer for each question.

This old, brick firehouse is red. It is also crowded. There are too many tools to fit on the shelf. There are hoses piled everywhere. People bump into each other inside the firehouse. It was built a long time ago. There were fewer homes to protect back then. It is time to get a bigger firehouse!

1. What is the main idea of this paragraph?
   a. The old firehouse is red.
   b. The old firehouse was built a long time ago.
   c. The old firehouse is too small.
2. Choose two details that tell about the main idea.
   a. The firehouse has piles of hoses.
   b. The firehouse is made from bricks.
   c. People bump into each other inside it.
3. Which detail does not talk about the main idea?
   a. There are too many tools to fit on the shelf.
   b. The firehouse is red.
   c. People bump into each other inside the firehouse.
4. Suggest an appropriate title for this passage.

C. The child in the poem 'Sick' wants to take a holiday from school. March 26 is 'Make Your Own Holiday Day'. You can make this day a special day for any reason you want. **Make a holiday of your own. Then, write a paragraph about how you will celebrate it.**

D. 'The Incident of the Letter' and 'The Barber's Wife' are stories about a doctor and a barber.

Form pairs. One student will think of a profession, write it on a piece of paper and stick the paper on another student's back. The other student must guess what profession it is by asking only 'yes/no' questions.

13

An Old Friend

Jayanti Adhikari

Let's Get Started

The United Nations Sustainable Development Goal 15 is about life on land. It states that we must stop the loss of forest land that the growth of cities causes.

Tick (✓) the sentences that tell you Iman cares for life around her. Mark a cross (×) against things that she does which are harmful for the environment.

- I am learning how to compost dry leaves, fruit and vegetable peels, and other kitchen waste. ☐
- I plant a tree every year on my birthday. ☐
- I leave the tap on while brushing my teeth. ☐

- I use a plastic watering can because I don't think plastic is harmful for the environment. ☐
- I pluck flowers from the local park because I enjoy their beauty. ☐
- I borrow books from the library instead of buying new ones. I do this to protect our forests. ☐
- I switch off lights and fans when I leave a room. ☐

Learning and Awareness: Coexistence in society and nature

Reading

Have you ever given names to the trees and plants growing in and around your house?

This is a tale of a boy and a neem tree his grandfather had planted. Find out what happens when the tree was struck by lightning.

Shyamal was looking **affectionately** at the neem tree from his bed. He had been in bed with typhoid for a month and Nimai had been his companion through that time. He could hardly think of a more comforting sight than the handsome and elegant tree holding its head high against the background of the blue sky. He could almost hear his grandfather's voice in the **murmur** of the small green leaves and the long, spreading branches. Grandpa would often tell him how people believed that a few drops of heavenly **nectar** fell on the neem tree, giving it medicinal properties.

Shyamal's grandfather planted the neem tree on the day their family came to live in the newly built house. Although Shyamal was not born at that time, he imagined his young grandfather entering the house, smiling **triumphantly**. In his hand was the neem plant, which he had collected from the old gardener in his office.

Since then, Nimai, as the tree was named, had been a part of their lives. It was the place for Grandfather's morning prayers. The neighbourhood remembered his gentle, **rhythmic** voice chanting the ***surya pranam***. In summer, he would come and sit under the tree as the afternoon breeze started. How he loved to see the neem flowers appearing from March to April, the air carrying their light **fragrance** and the greenish-yellow fruits ripening from June to August. For hours, he would sit there reading, writing or gazing at the **numerous** young leaves, and the birds and squirrels who lived in it.

He could talk endlessly about the uses of every part of the tree. The seed oil and soap could be used for various skin diseases. The bark was used as **tincture**. Shyamal's grandmother always kept dried neem leaves in between books and clothes to protect them from **weevils**. A favourite family dish was neem leaves fried with small pieces of brinjal.

affectionately: in a way that shows fondness

murmur: a continuous low sound

nectar: (here) a liquid which the gods drink

triumphantly: in a way that shows pride and happiness as if after a victory

rhythmic: repeated at regular intervals

surya pranam: a Sanskrit chant devoted to the sun god, Surya

fragrance: a sweet smell

numerous: many

tincture: a medicine consisting of alcohol and a small amount of a drug

weevils: small insects which feed on grain and seeds and destroy crops

In his childhood, Grandfather had once had smallpox. His mother used to comfort his burning skin with the feather light touch of neem leaves. He often told Shyamal, his most devoted listener, that the neem leaves still reminded him of his mother's affectionate touch.

Shyamal always remembered the day when the news came of Grandmother's death at his uncle's house in Mysore. The old man didn't utter a word, but sat all day under the tree, perhaps looking at his age-old companion for strength.

Grandfather left their family just as suddenly and silently. Shyamal had been sent to call in Grandfather, who had been sitting under the neem tree all evening. At first, Shyamal had thought he was dozing and had tried to wake him up. 'Grandfather, your time of chatting with Nimai is up.' But the old man's head fell to his chest at Shyamal's touch. As Shyamal stood, shocked, he noticed a few dried neem leaves **flutter** down to Grandfather's lap.

That had been a few months ago. Shyamal was a thoughtful boy, much like his grandfather. The loss had **affected** him deeply. This afternoon, he was **lost in his thoughts**, looking at Nimai's shiny leaves.

His mother came in with the news of the day. 'The new car your father talked about will be delivered this evening.'

This was great news indeed and the boy was very excited. He jumped down from his bed and announced, 'I am not going to stay in bed any more. This very evening, I am going on a long drive with Papa.'

When the first rush of excitement was over, his mother broke the next piece of news to Shyamal **cautiously**, 'Your father says that we have to cut down Nimai to make place for a garage for the car.'

Shyamal could not believe his ears. 'How can you do that? Would you get rid of me or Banani because of lack of space? Don't you remember how much Grandpa loved the tree?' The fourteen-year-old boy's voice was lost in sobs.

Shyamal's mother called his father. There was a long argument between father and son on the phone, but the boy would not budge.

'You are just being stubborn, son. Your grandfather was my father. I loved him too. We can remember him in a hundred other ways. And where else can we keep the car?' his father asked.

flutter: move through the air with small, quick movements

affected: changed in some way

lost in his thoughts: not aware of what is happening around him

cautiously: carefully

In the end, he **decreed** that the woodcutters would come the next morning, whether Shyamal liked it or not.

Shyamal was left to himself for the rest of the day. The house was busy and nobody seemed to notice the **morose** boy. Towards evening, the sky was dark with heavy rain clouds. There was a **clap of thunder** and big drops of rain started to fall. The fragrance of wet soil reminded Shyamal of his grandfather and the way he took in deep breaths of the rain-soaked air.

Suddenly, there was a **deafening** sound. The lights in the house went off and a bright flash lit up the world outside for a second. When his eyes adjusted themselves to the darkness, Shyamal saw that Nimai was burning and heard his father scream from somewhere near the gate. This was too much for the boy who had been a bundle of anxiety from the expected loss of his beloved tree. His head spun as he sank to the ground.

When he opened his eyes, he saw his family looking at him. His father held him in his arms. There were tears in his eyes. Later, they told him that a big bolt of lightning had struck the tree. Had it not been for Nimai, it would have struck his father as he got out from the car. Even as the tree died, it performed a last act of kindness to the family.

The next morning, Shyamal was not in his room. A note on his table said that he was going out with their old servant, Prasad.

As the day wore on, his parents got more and more anxious. Shyamal's father, his uncles and friends went out to search for him at his friends' homes, and then in hospitals and police stations. But there was no news to be had. A fourteen-year-old boy and an old servant seemed to have vanished from the city.

It was almost 10:30 at night. The lights **blazed** in every room. The **extended family** filled the house, but nobody spoke.

Suddenly, somebody shouted, 'There he is!' Everyone rushed out. Shyamal could be seen at a distance, followed

Did You Know? Science

The botanical name of the neem tree, *Azadirachta indica*, comes from a Persian description of the tree *azad darakht-i-Hindil*. It literally means 'the free tree of India'.

decreed: decided

morose: sad and bad-tempered

clap of thunder: the deep rumbling sound heard in the sky after a flash of lightning

deafening: very loud

blazed: lighted up excessively brightly

extended family: a family group that includes relatives such as uncles, aunts and grandparents, as well as parents and children

by Prasad. The boy had walked a long way. His face **gleamed** with sweat, and dust covered his knees. But his face was lit up with a triumphant smile. He held a small neem sapling in his hands.

gleamed: shined

Everybody began questioning him at once, but he only answered his mother. 'Ma, I found Grandfather's old gardener's house with the help of Prasad uncle. Now, this sapling will take Nimai's place.' His face shone with the love which his grandfather had passed on to him.

Comprehension

Quick Recap

A. Answer the questions in a few lines.

1. List the uses of the neem tree.
2. Why was Nimai a favourite of Shyamal's grandfather?
3. Why did Shyamal's father want to cut down the neem tree?
4. Why was Shyamal against cutting down Nimai?
5. What eventually happened to the neem tree?
6. Why did Shyamal disappear with his servant? Where did he go?

B. Read the lines from the story and answer the questions.

1. *His mother used to comfort him with the feather light touch of the neem leaves.*
   a. Who is being referred to as 'he' here?
   b. What had happened to him?
   c. What did the neem leaves remind him of later in his life?
2. *'How can you do that?'*
   a. Who said this and to whom?
   b. What action of the listener is being referred to here?
   c. How did it make the speaker feel?

Life Skills and Values — saving the environment

Think and answer.

1. What kind of a person is Shyamal? Do you think there are any similarities between Shyamal and his grandfather?
2. Do you think cutting down Nimai would have been the right thing to do?
3. Do you think trees protect us from natural calamities and disasters? Discuss in context of the story.

21ST CENTURY Information Literacy

Way with Words

Polite Requests in the Form of Questions

In English, requests can be made in the form of questions using words such as **will**, **shall**, **would**, **should**, **could**, **may** and **might**.

Example: **Will** you please come with me to watch the match?

A. Form polite requests by underlining the correct options.

1. *Could/Couldn't/Won't/Wouldn't* you open the window, please? It's hot in here.
2. *Could you/Will you/Would you* mind buying two loaves of bread on your way home?
3. Would you mind if I *borrowed/will borrow/would borrow* your dictionary for an hour?
4. Would you mind if I *didn't/won't/wouldn't* come to your party?
5. *Would/Could/Wouldn't/Couldn't* you get me a glass of water, please?

B. Work in pairs and practise making these requests.

1. You want to go on a school trip. Ask your parents.
2. You want to take part in the debate competition. Ask your teacher.
3. You lose your way to the park. You seek the help of a passer-by.
4. You are going out while it is raining. You want to borrow your friend's umbrella.

Grammar in Use

Inappropriate Shift in Verb Tense

If a sentence describes two actions, of which one happens after the other, the tense of the verbs must be consistent and should not be mixed.

Example: After Rameez **left** the academy, he *goes* to the gym every evening. (inappropriate shift)
After Rameez **leaves** the academy, he *goes* to the gym every evening. (correct verb tense)

A. State whether the following sentences are correct or incorrect. Rewrite the incorrect sentences after correcting the mistakes.

1. I don't like this sofa because it sagged.
2. We will buy a new fridge if this one breaks down.

3. Please make your bed before you go to school.
4. We had sandwiches for breakfast and we will had pizza for dinner.
5. I finish my homework and now I was going to watch TV.
6. Raghav brings cupcakes to school whenever he feels like.
7. We will be playing chess when the lights went off.
8. Remember to take your umbrella as it will have been raining since morning.

Comparison of Adverbs

Just like adjectives, adverbs also have three degrees of comparison: **positive**, **comparative** and **superlative**.

We use **more** to form the comparative and **most** to form the superlative forms of adverbs that end in **-ly**.

Examples: Shyamal was looking **affectionately** at the neem tree from his bed.

affectionately (positive)	more affectionately (comparative)	most affectionately (superlative)

We use **-er** to form the comparative form and **-est** to form the superlative form with adverbs that do not end in **-ly**.

Examples: Grandfather worked **hard** to build this house.

hard (positive)	harder (comparative)	hardest (superlative)

However, some adverbs have irregular comparative and superlative forms.

Examples: little	less	least
badly	worse	worst

B. Fill in the blanks with the comparative or superlative form of the given adverbs.

clearly quietly quickly extremely melodiously carefully well fluently

1. Jatin finished his lunch ____________ than his brother and went out to play.
2. She speaks English ____________ than Russian.
3. The children behaved ____________ than usual under the teacher's supervision.
4. Pari sings the ____________ in the class.
5. Our football team played ____________ than the other school team.
6. Most patients wish doctors would write ____________.
7. After the accident last year he drives ____________.
8. He is ____________ gentle, he can't even hurt a fly.

Study Skills

Pronounce Well

Pronunciation of Words with Letter 'u'

The letter 'u' can produce six different sounds based on its position and its surrounding letters in a word.

Read out the words given in the box and divide them according to the different sounds of u.

burial	abacus	business	sun	blue	dull
occur	blur	bush	bull	pull	tube

u as in put	u as in muse	u as in fur	u as in focus	u as in busy	u as in bury	u as in cut

Listening and Speaking

Listen to the medicinal properties of the neem tree. There are many other plants whose leaves are used to cure illnesses.

Example: Basil (tulsi) is used as a medicine for cold.

Research and speak on one such plant or tree in the class. Describe the plant and its medicinal properties.

You can answer the following questions:

- What is the plant's scientific name?
- Where is it commonly found?
- Which parts of the plant are used?
- Which diseases can it cure?

HC Coexistence in society and Nature

Pen it Down

Imagine you are Shyamal. Write a diary entry on the day you went out with Prasad to find a neem sapling.

You can use the following points:

- why you left without informing your family
- problems you faced while finding the gardener's house
- people you met on the way
- how you felt after finding the tree
- how you brought the tree back

Self Assessment

Now I can

- read a story about how trees and plants can be a source of happiness.
- correct inappropriate shift in tenses and understand the comparison of adjectives.
- research and speak on a given topic, and pronounce words with *o* sound.
- make polite requests and write a diary entry.

Read More

Ellie, the Evergreen: This story by Jean Warren is about the tree, Ellie the Evergreen, a tree that is sad in the autumn season when other trees change colour. However, when winter arrives, Ellie becomes the most beautiful tree in the park.

The Giving Tree: This book by Shel Silverstein is about the relation between a boy and an apple tree as they grow up together.

short story

14

Shall We Ghost

Spooks and the Supernatural

H. A. Manhood

Let's Get Started

Many cultures have stories about ghosts and the supernatural. For example, the famous 'Vikram and Betal' stories are about a brave king who is forced to carry a ghost on his back and listen to its stories every night.

Find and highlight the words related to ghosts in the word grid. Use the help box.

B	C	A	F	R	A	I	D	O	S	P
V	G	O	D	A	A	B	A	S	U	A
S	H	R	I	E	K	D	R	F	S	B
A	Z	L	C	F	L	G	K	W	P	M
A	C	R	E	A	K	C	A	C	E	K
A	H	A	B	G	L	C	X	C	N	L
S	I	S	N	H	K	V	Z	Y	S	W
K	L	A	C	K	U	T	F	V	E	E
D	L	D	M	A	A	Y	A	U	D	R
F	S	F	J	N	S	P	O	O	K	Y
S	E	G	L	S	R	H	I	I	S	R
P	R	H	K	C	T	S	K	P	V	T
I	T	J	H	A	U	P	T	E	D	T
R	Y	K	A	R	Y	I	F	O	B	Y
I	U	L	A	Y	O	R	A	J	A	R
T	O	G	H	O	S	T	L	Y	X	A

afraid, shriek, spooky, dark, creak, scary, ghostly, suspense, chills, spirit

HC **Learning and Awareness:** Humans and other orders

Reading

Have you ever wondered if ghosts exist? In this story, a very old house has been put up for sale. Strange things start happening on the day the household items are being

auctioned off. Find out what happens at the auction.

Presamber Grance was for sale, ghost and all, but I did not hear about it until the day the furniture was to be **auctioned**. I had once lunched with the head of the family and she had promised to leave me the pair of carved **cherubs** hanging at the top of the winding stairs.

There was still a chance that I could buy the cherubs. The head porter was busy captaining the sale but not too busy to pocket ten **shillings** and tell me that the cherubs were not included in the **catalogue**. Maybe they were among the piled rubbish in one of the **attic** rooms. I was free to look, provided I did not obstruct the sale, and if I found them we could settle privately without undue **accountancy**.

A machine-shop hum and shuffle came from the great drawing room, broken by the irregular rap of the auctioneer's **gavel**, but the rest of the house was quiet. All except the bedroom on the first floor. From this came the sound of heart-broken sobbing. I pushed open the door and saw a child kneeling by a chair near an open window, sniffing and gulping. She must have been about seven years old, plain and **freckled**, her sandy hair plaited tightly and linked at the ends with black tape. She looked up crossly.

'Go away!'

'And why should I?'

'Because I never want to see anyone again. I want to die. I hate everybody.'

'And why?'

'Because everything's spoilt.'

'But not past mending, surely? Come now, tell me about it. Then perhaps we can do something. What's your name?'

She looked at me suspiciously, deciding fiercely to tell, her fists tight and her thin body **bitterly** stiff.

auctioned: sold to the person who offered the highest price in a public sale

cherubs: angels that look like children with wings

shillings: a unit of money used in Britain till 1971

catalogue: a list of items written in a systematic manner

attic: a room at the top of a house just below the roof

accountancy: complex process of making a payment

gavel: a small wooden hammer that the person in charge of an auction holds

freckled: covered with small light brown spots on the face

bitterly: in a way that shows anger or dislike

Her name was Rowena and her aunt was the housekeeper. She had lived at Presamber since her mother died. It was a beautiful, wonderful house and she never wanted to live anywhere else. She would never go back and live in the ugly town where she came from; she would rather die and make them all very, very sorry.

'But have you tried to do something about it? Why not ask the ghost to help? If it won't, become a temporary ghost yourself. Have a shot at stopping the sale, scaring the crowd away and frightening the crowd to death.' It seemed better that she should have an idea to play with than to sit and feel sorry.

To my surprise, she responded whole-heartedly. She stopped sniffing and said, 'So I will! I'll ghost them all away. I'll make them cry and run and be very sorry. Good bye!'

Briskly, she slid from the chair, edging past me into the passage, running upstairs two at a time, pigtails bobbing. I followed more slowly, wondering how and where she would begin the ghosting. I lost her on the third landing. 'Perhaps for the best,' I thought and went looking for the cherubs.

Selling was brisk in the drawing room, the crowd thick and merry. I pushed my way inside and **regretted** at once. As if my coming was a signal, the dealers grouped by the huge fireplace scattered suddenly, coughing and swearing as **soot billowed** outwards into the room. Not a little soot either, but repeated falls of it as if eagles had just then decided to nest in the chimney and were cleaning the house first. I guessed that Rowena had gone into action. It wasn't a bad beginning either. Clothes were blackened and faces **smudged**. When the fog cleared, people began to sneeze.

briskly: quickly

regretted: felt bad about something one had done or failed to do

soot: black powder that rises in the smoke from a fire and collects on the inside of chimneys

billowed: rose and moved in a large quantity

smudged: made dirty

Wordwise

The word 'auction' comes from the Latin word *auctus*, which means increasing.

I wondered what Rowena's next move would be. Soon, a loud scream interrupted the auctioneer as he described the beauties of a most ugly vase. The porter dropped the vase in astonishment. The scream had come from an old lady seated on a couch. Mice had run over her, she complained tremblingly. The auctioneer said 'nonsense', then stopped, as a mouse ran across his table and scurried out of sight. Half a dozen women left hurriedly, muttering in terror, and the room echoed to the stamp of pursuing feet. Mentally, I congratulated Rowena, wondering where she had got the mice from. I looked for her, intending to **recommend** the soft pedal, but she was nowhere to be seen.

Somewhat **one-leggedly**, the sale proceeded. The auctioneer knocked down several lots rapidly to restore confidence. The tension had begun to ease when a peculiar smell, as of last year's eggs and **festering** whales, filled the room. Boldly, the auctioneer ignored the smell, flapping the paper **indifferently**. He regained their attention, but once more, eyes looked away from him, this time upwards. Slowly, like a patiently drawn map, a damp patch appeared on the ceiling and water began to drip.

At his best, the auctioneer was not a handsome man. Now, he had a boiled, **soggy** look, the sharp bones of his face projecting whitely. He ordered a porter to find the leak and spoke a stern warning to those who seemed determined to ruin the sale. Rowena must have been listening, for there immediately came the **frenzied twanging** on **harps**.

The auctioneer stood up, hammering furiously. So furiously that he hit an inkwell and splashed himself and his clerk most thoroughly.

'The police! Fetch the police!'

recommend: suggest
one-leggedly: (here) half-heartedly
festering: rotting
indifferently: without showing any concern
soggy: wet
frenzied: wild, excited
twanging: pulling and releasing strings
harps: large musical instruments consisting of a row of strings
heaved: (here) rushed while pushing away those who were around
jamming: blocking
souvenirs: things kept as a reminder of a person, a place or an event
feathering: flowing out
inspiration: (here) new idea

But he hadn't a chance, for an overriding cry came from somewhere above: 'Fire!' Those still remaining **heaved** in panic, **jamming** the doorway. The brighter ones climbed out through the windows, several of them gathering up **souvenirs** as they went.

Guiltily, I followed them, determined never to put ideas into young heads. The house was alight, smoke **feathering** from the upper windows and the roof. I looked for Rowena, praying she hadn't mentioned the source of **inspiration**.

Soon, the fire engine arrived. There seemed no point in staying, especially as two constables had begun questioning everyone in sight. I had left the car in a lane at the back of the house. It was there that I found Rowena, **placidly** garlanding a collection of dolls with flowers, singing to herself, undisturbed by the distant **clamour** or the **wispy** ash drifting down like the floss of spent blossom. I looked at her in admiration blended with horror and a sense of responsibility.

'You certainly made a good job of the ghosting with soot and mice, water and fire,' I said.

She looked up suspiciously, replying: 'It wasn't me. I did empty some paint down the stairs, but then Aunt told me we were going to live in a much nicer house with a river running through the garden. So I didn't bother anymore.'

It all felt peculiarly complicated, especially when I got back to the car and found the two cherubs lying on the back seat, each with a ripe cherry in its mouth, which was in itself remarkable, for the month was September and cherries were long gone.

placidly: calmly

clamour: the loud noise of a large group of people talking or shouting together

wispy: fine; not thick

About the author

Harold Alfred Manhood (1904–1991) usually wrote stories that have a rural setting where supernatural events take place. He is noted for his collection of short stories like *Nightseed and Other Tales, Apples by Night* and *Fierce and Gentle.*

Comprehension

Quick Recap

A. Answer the questions in a few lines.

1. What did the narrator want to take back with him from the auction at Presamber Grance?
2. Why did the narrator bribe the porter?
3. Why was Rowena sobbing profusely?
4. What advice did the narrator give to Rowena?
5. What were the strange incidents happening in the house that day?

B. Read these lines from the story and answer the questions.

1. *'But have you tried to do something about it?'*
   a. Who said this and to whom?
   b. What was the speaker referring to?
   c. What were the speaker's suggestions to the listener?
2. *'You certainly made a good job of the ghosting with soot and mice, water and fire.'*
   a. Who said this and to whom?
   b. Who was behind all the pranks?
   c. Why was the speaker left confused by the end of it?

Life Skills and Values reasoning

Think and answer.

1. Describe the things that created an atmosphere of strangeness about Presamber Grance.
2. Do you think the narrator was right in telling Rowena to act like a ghost and frighten people away?
3. Who do you think was responsible for all the strange happenings that took place at Presamber Grance on the day of the auction?

21ST CENTURY Critical Thinking

Way with Words

A. Read the descriptions of the different parts of a house and complete their names.

1. flat roof of a house	T __ R __ __ C __
2. covered entrance of a house	P O __ __ __
3. platform projecting from a building	B __ L C __ __ Y
4. small room within the roof of a house	A T __ __ C
5. small private road leading up to a house	D __ I V __ W __ __
6. small entrance room in a house	F O __ __ R
7. underground room used for storage	C __ L __ __ R
8. small room near the kitchen where kitchenware and food rations are kept	P A __ __ R __

B. Make sentences with any four words from exercise A.

Grammar in Use

Modals

Modals are special verbs which are used with other verbs to express ability, possibility, permission and obligation.

Look at this table to understand the uses of the various modals.

Modals	Uses	Examples
can	ability to do something	I **can** speak English.
	permission to do something	**Can** I go to play?
	request or suggestion	**Can** you wait a moment, please?
	offer	I **can** lend you my book till tomorrow
	possibility	It **can** get very cold in Shimla.
may	possibility	It **may** rain today.
	permission to do something	**May** I go to play?
	polite suggestion	**May** I help you?
might/ must	possibility (less possible than *may*)	It **might** rain today.
	force, necessity	I **must** sleep early tonight.
	possibility	You **must** be tired.
	advice, recommendation	You **must** study well.
will	wish, request, demand, order	**Will** you please shut the door?
	prediction, assumption	I think it **will** rain tonight.
	promise	I **will** study harder.
	habits	She **will** sit for hours without talking.

A. Fill in the blanks with appropriate modals.

1. My grandmother is eighty-five-years old, but she ____________ still read and write without glasses. (ability)
2. ____________ I come with you? (permission)
3. ____________ you help me with the housework, please? (polite request)
4. It is snowing outside, so you ____________ stay at home. (necessity)
5. I ____________ get you a shawl from Kashmir. (promise)
6. China ____________ become a super power by 2025. (possibility)
7. ____________ you take care of my dog for a day? (polite request)
8. It's very cold today. Do you think it ____________ snow later? (possibility)

Punctuation

Read the sentences and note the situations where capital letters are used.

I never want to see anyone again. (the personal pronoun *I*)

I like watching programmes on the **BBC**. (abbreviations and acronyms)

The girl's birthday was next **Wednesday**, that is, on 25 **D**ecember, which was also **C**hristmas. (days of the week, months of the year and holidays)

Hindi is spoken in many parts of India. (languages and countries)

Many **S**ri **L**ankans are followers of **B**uddhism. (nationalities and religions)

Professor **J**ain likes teaching **S**hakespeare's plays. (names and titles)

They visited **B**uckingham **P**alace during their holiday. (places and monuments)

We watched ***T**he **S**ound of **M**usic* yesterday. (titles of books, poems, plays and films)

The **comma** is used for a short pause, to separate words and to separate word groups in a list. **Examples:** If you need my help, write to me.
We brought apples, oranges, bananas, and grapes.

The **full stop** (.) is used to indicate the end of a sentence.

Example: The film was quite good.

The **question mark** (?) is placed at the end of questions.

Example: Can you help me with my luggage?

The **exclamation mark** (!) is used at the end of an exclamatory sentence.

Example: What a sad story!

B. Correct the punctuation errors in the following paragraph.

once upon a time there was a girl not more than eight years of age who loved to tell tall tales. since she told tales very often nobody ever believed a word she said. therefore it was no surprise that nobody listened one day when she cried 'my grandfather's house is on fire!' everyone in the village laughed as she begged cried and pleaded for someone to follow her after a few minutes one woman said 'Should we see if the house is really burning' at that moment someone spotted smoke immediately the villagers headed to the burning house they got sand a hose pipe and water to help extinguish the flames. This frightening incident convinced the child that lying was not a good habit.

Study Skills

Spell Check

Underline the correct spelling in each set.

1. dependant	dependent	depandent
2. license	licence	licens

3. occurence ocurrence occurrence
4. seperate separate separete
5. comittee committee commitee
6. playwright playwrite playrite

Listening and Speaking

Listen to the expressions used to put forth an opinion and the expressions used to agree or disagree with an opinion.

Now, imagine that you are attending an auction with a friend. You want to buy one of the items on sale and share your opinion about it. In pairs, enact two conversations. In one, your friend agrees with and appreciates your choice. In the other, they disagree with your choice because they think the item is worthless. Use the expressions you just heard.

Pen it Down

Write a short scary story beginning with:

One night it was raining and I was alone at home when I heard footsteps in the next room …

Self Assessment

Now I can

- read and enjoy a story about inexplicable incidents in a house.
- practise modals and use punctuation marks correctly.
- express an opinion and respond to an opinion.
- write a short scary story.

Read More

The Fall of the House of Usher: This story by Edgar Allan Poe is about a brother and a sister living in their old family house. The house, which seems to have a life of its own, falls down at the same time as the siblings die.

Haunted: This is a ghost story by Harris Tobias that tells the story of an old haunted house. The ghosts in the story love to bake and party.

Nature

15

Rain in the Hills

Rehana Ali

Let's Get Started

Do you like the rain or do you feel that it makes you gloomy and sad? Here are some pictures depicting words related to rain. Identify the words, and in one sentence, state a personal experience related to each of these natural phenomena.

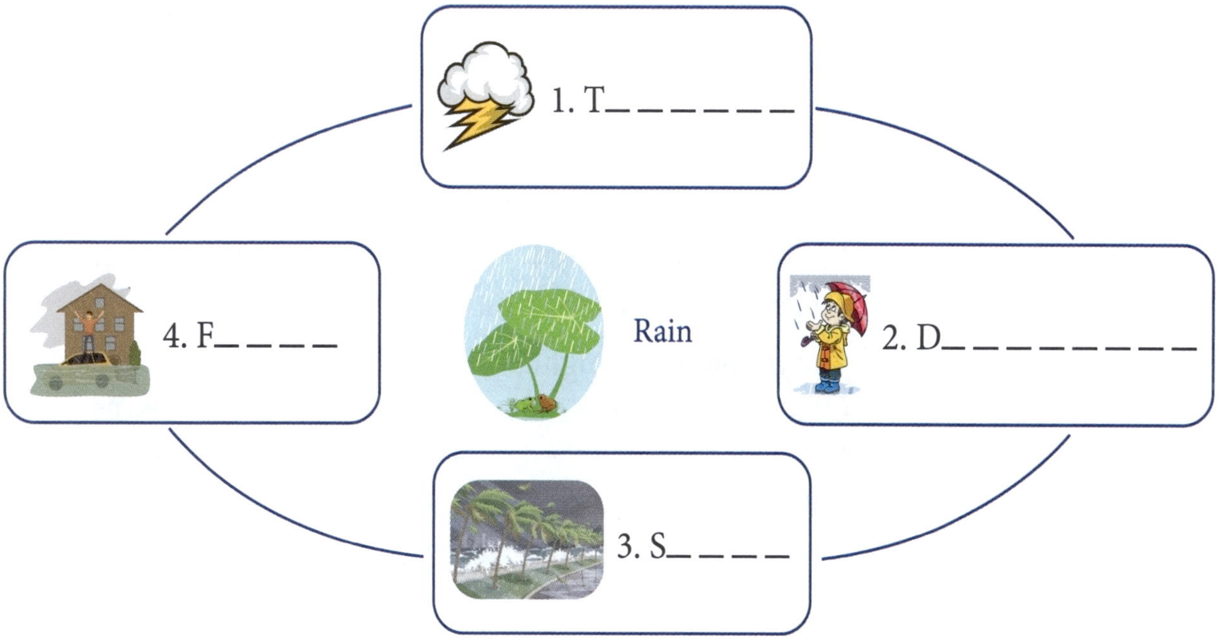

1. a loud noise that accompanies lightning before or during rain
2. light rain falling in fine drops
3. very bad weather, with heavy rain, strong winds, and often thunder and lightning
4. a phenomenon in which water overflows from rivers and covers land causing great harm

HC **Learning and Awareness:** Momentary and deeper happiness

Reading

Have you ever travelled in the hills by bus, when it was raining heavily? How did it feel?

Read this poem about the impressions of a hill station in the rain during heavy rain.

slender: slim
drizzle: very light rain
breathtaking: very exciting
heady: strong and attractive
rolling thunder: deep sound caused by thunder
cascading: coming down in waves
enthralls: holds spellbound
murky: gloomy or dark
menacing: threatening
trundles: moves heavily
serpentine: curved like a snake
gorge: a deep valley through which a river runs
ravine: deep narrow steep-sided valley formed by running water
hearth: the floor of a fireplace
wane: decrease gradually
pine: (here) to feel a great longing or desire for something

The rocky paths,
The **slender** trees,
The gentle **drizzle,**
The heavenly breeze.

The ice cool water
Of a mountain spring,
The scent of rain
Making crickets sing.

The **breathtaking** view
Of the valley below,
The **heady** pine fragrance,
Wherever I go.

The fog that hides
The view from my eyes,
The snowcapped peaks,
The golden sunrise.

The **rolling thunder**
Announcing a storm,
Birds huddled in nests
To keep themselves warm.

The thunderous might
Of a **cascading** fall,
Fed by the rain,
Enthralls one and all.

High over the peaks
A lone eagle flies,
Its wings spread across
The grey **murky** skies.

The magnificent pines sway
On a dark windy night
That lights up in flashes,
Of silvery-white

The rain beats down
On cliffs sheer and steep,
The **menacing** slopes,
The valley so deep.

My bus **trundles** on, on
Its path **serpentine**
My eyes are glued
To the **gorge** and **ravine**

Far away at a distance
Village homes on a slope
Their twinkling **hearths**
Fill me with hope.

The hills have a magic
That never can **wane**
I **pine** to go back
Again and again.

About the poet

Rehana Ali is a teacher who lives and teaches in Lucknow.

Comprehension

Quick Recap

A. Answer the questions in a few lines.

1. What is the theme of the poem?
2. What hides the view of the poet?
3. Which line in the poem uses personification?

B. Read the lines from the poem and answer the questions.

1. *The rolling thunder*
   Announcing a storm
   a. What is being referred to here?
   b. What is the thunder announcing?
   c. How do other animals react to the sound of thunder?
2. *My bus trundles on and on*
   Its path serpentine
   a. Why do you think the bus 'trundles on and on'?
   b. Why is the path referred to as serpentine?
   c. What does the poet see while the bus trundles on?

Life Skills and Values — appreciating nature

Think and answer.

1. Is the tone of the poem happy or sad?
2. Why do you think the 'twinkling hearths' give the poet hope?
3. Is the poet going to the hills or away from them? Give reasons for your answer.

Way with Words

Sense Words

The poem uses many words and phrases related to the senses of sight, smell, hearing, taste and touch.

Examples: The ice cool water
Of a mountain spring, (*touch*)
The scent of rain (*smell*)
Making crickets sing. (*hearing*)

Categorise the following words according to the five senses that they relate to.

1. smooth
2. bitter
3. colourful
4. shrill
5. grainy
6. quiet
7. slimy
8. bright
9. slippery
10. dark
11. silent
12. sweet
13. rough
14. salty
15. deaf
16. wet

Grammar in Use

'IN' AND 'INTO'

The preposition **in** is used to describe where someone or something already is.

Example: The students are **in** the classroom.

The preposition **into** is used when something or someone is going or being put into another location. It is also used to show change.

Examples: The boy came running **into** the room.
The caterpillar changed **into** a butterfly.

Complete the sentences with in or into.

1. The tooth fairy put the child's tooth ____________ her pocket.
2. My friend dropped ____________ to say hello.
3. The frog jumped ____________ the well.
4. The diver dived ____________ the sea.
5. He had put the dish ____________ the oven for baking.
6. His small birthday party turned ____________ a huge bash.
7. If we are to win the match, we have to score 16 runs ____________ the last over.

Study Skills

Use Your Dictionary

WORDS RELATED TO TRAIN TRAVEL

Match the words related to train travel to their meanings.

1. porter •	• a. a room at the railway station where people can wait
2. waiting room •	• b. a machine that checks a traveller's luggage
3. station master •	• c. a person who checks tickets of passengers in a train
4. luggage scanner •	• d. a person who carries luggage at a railway station
5. berth •	• e. a place to sleep on, in a train
6. ticket collector •	• f. an official who is in charge of a railway station

Listening and Speaking

Listen to some words and repeat them slowly. Notice the sound made by the vowel in each word. Then, classify them as short vowel sounds and long vowel sounds.

Pen it Down

Imagine that it is the rainy season in your city. Write a report for a newspaper describing the conditions in your city. You can use the following points:

- waterlogging and traffic jams, frequent breakdowns of power and telephone lines
- shortage of vegetables, fruits and other essential items
- difficulty in taking sick people to hospitals
- the response and help from the local government authorities

Self Assessment

Now I can

- read and enjoy a poem about the beauty of rains in the hills.
- use sense words and understand the usage of the prepositions *in* and *into*.
- match words related to train travel and write a newspaper report.

Read More

The Voice of the Rain: This poem by Walt Whitman is in the form of a conversation between the speaker and the raindrops. The poem shows how rain takes care of life on earth.

The Rainy Day: This poem by H. W. Longfellow compares a dark rainy day to a bad phase in the poet's life. The poem talks about how even the saddest days are followed by happier times.

16

Pepper, the Phantom Pet–I

Paro Anand

Let's Get Started

A. Some words related to laughter are jumbled up. Unjumble and write them in the space given.

1. gilegg: __________
2. fugawf: __________
3. cohtler: __________
4. tertti: __________
5. blely glahu: _____ _____
6. kuchlec: __________

B. Complete these idioms related to laughter with the correct prepositions.

burst __________ laughing

roared __________ laughter

dissolve __________ laughter

crack __________

be __________ stitches

laugh your head __________

Feelings: Practising collaboration without competition

Reading

Do you know what a white lie is? A harmless lie is called a white lie. In the play, Pia tells a white lie. Read the play to find out what happens next.

Characters

Teacher: a young teacher who cannot control the class

Pallavi: a student, very tall and well-built, with an air of authority

Pia: a student, bright and quick

Principal: a large, **congenial** man, a little confused, with a loud voice

Avik: Pia's older brother, also very bright and quick

Other students

> congenial: pleasant
>
> chaotic: in a state of complete confusion and disorder
>
> pandemonium: state of extreme disorder and confusion

Scene opens in a classroom. It is ***chaotic****. There is much shouting, scraping of chairs and flinging of papers and pencils. General classroom* ***pandemonium.*** *The teacher enters, looks helplessly at the scene. Then walks in bravely, with a smile.*

Teacher (*With false brightness*) Good morning, children!

A moment's pause in the activities.

Students (*In a drone*) Good morning, Mrs Chawla!

Then the chaos continues.

Student 1 (*Trying to grab a pen that Student 2 is playing with*) Oye, that's mine! Give it back.

Student 2 Just keep quiet, okay, it's mine.

Student 3 Ya, what a liar, Arushi, it's his. Don't try and rob someone else's property.

Student 1 Don't lie, you don't even know anything. Give it back, it's mine.

Students start throwing the pen around.

Student 1 Ma'am! Look, they're stealing my things, they're always stealing my ...

Student 4 Ma'am, what are we going to do today?

Student 5 Ma'am, ma'am, ma'am, let's do something really fun, ma'am.

Students Yes, let's do something fun, ma'am. Please ma'am. It's so boring, ma'am. No writing, ma'am, please. Let's go on a picnic, ma'am!

There is much cheering at this last suggestion. The noise ***escalates*** *and the teacher is getting very* ***flustered****, trying to get them to quiet down. Finally, Pallavi comes to her rescue.*

Wordwise

The famous poet, Milton, coined the word 'pandemonium' in his poem *Paradise Lost*. The literal meaning of pandemonium is 'the place of all demons'. With time, its meaning evolved to mean confusion, disorder or uproar.

Pallavi Hey come on, keep quiet. Can't you see that ma'am's waiting for us? Behave yourselves.

Slowly the class settles down. Everyone sits, while Pallavi stands, hands on her waist, like a thug. Someone tries to start making a noise, but Pallavi turns to them and they stop immediately.

Pallavi (*Turning to the teacher triumphantly*) Go ahead, ma'am, you can continue with your lesson.

Teacher (*With a smile at Pallavi*) Now, children, today we are going to discuss domestic animals.

Immediately, the class is ***rocked*** *by a storm of protests. Only Pia stands and cheers.*

escalates: increases

flustered: nervous and confused

rocked: (here) shook

hutch: a box or cage for keeping small animals

Students No, no! That's so boring! Pia, stop being an animal for once! Ya, just because you are the big animal expert! No, ma'am, nothing about animals. We did that in class 1. Let's do something else, pleeease! Let's go for a picnic!

Another round of cheering at this suggestion.

Pallavi Hey, come on guys, that's enough!

Teacher As I was saying, children, today we have to talk about domestic animals and just to make it interesting, I thought, let's start by each one of you telling us about the pets you may have at home. We'll start with you, Pallavi.

Pallavi Yeah, as most of the lucky ones who've been to my house know, I've got a **hutch** full of rare angora rabbits. They are very beautiful and they have this long soft fur, so people breed them for the fur, to make sweaters.

Students Yeah ma'am, the fur's so soft, ma'am.

Teacher Very good, Pallavi! Who's next?

Many hands wave in the air and there are shouts of 'Ma'am me, ma'am me!'

Teacher Yes, Rohan?

Student 6 I've got the fiercest dog in the whole world, a **Rottweiler**. His name is Killer. He's a very dangerous dog, but he is highly trained, so he doesn't bite any of us. But you'd better not come near him, he'd kill you in one bite!

Teacher Thank you, Rohan. Next?

Student 2 I've got a pair of twin Persian cats. They are very, very highly **pedigreed** and my uncle says they are a very rare colour. I have to brush them every day. Their names are Silver and Gold because they're so precious. They ...

*The rest of the presentations take place in **mime**. Pia gets up and walks downstage to talk directly to the audience. She is troubled.*

Pia I'm in such trouble. What can I tell you? I'm supposed to be an animal expert who knows all about pets and training, dogs and wildlife. I talk about nothing else. So when my turn comes, they're going to want something special from me. You would think that such an animal expert would have a few **exotic** pets at home, right? Wrong! The only 'pet' I have, if you can call him that, is an ancient street dog, who wanders in and out of our house when he pleases, and who is more like a rug on the floor than a pet. We got him believing that **mutts** were good guard dogs, but he sleeps so soundly that you can drag him around by the collar, and he sleeps through it all. What am I going to do? They'll all laugh at me if I tell them about my silly dog.

Teacher Come on, Pia, stop daydreaming, let's hear about your pets.

*There is silence. Everyone turns to Pia in **anticipation**.*

Student 3 Yeah, Pia! What's your pet? Bet it's the best.

Student 4 Pia, the great animal expert! Go on, Pia, don't tell me you don't have a pet.

Rottweiler: a large powerful breed of dog

pedigreed: pure-bred

mime: the use of movements and gestures in order to express or tell something

exotic: (here) unusual and interesting because it comes from a distant country

mutt: a dog that is a mixture of different breeds

anticipation: feeling of excitement about something interesting that is about to happen

Student 5 She has a dog. I've seen it. It's a **mangy** old street dog, it can hardly walk!

Much laughter.

Student 1 Really Pia? Only a mangy dog?

Maybe it's a wolf in disguise. (***giggles** all around*)

Student 2 Shut up! Of course she has an exotic pet! No, Pia? Bet she has the most exciting pet.

Students Come on Pia, tell us!

Pia: (*to the audience*) See what I mean? So, you'll forgive me for what I'm going to do, won't you? I mean, you do understand that I have to? I have an image, a reputation to protect. I have to think of my fans. I don't want to let everybody down.

Pia goes slowly to the front of the class. As soon as she is there, everyone is quiet.

Teacher Go on, Pia, we'd love to hear all about your pet.

Pia (*Almost **inaudibly***) I have a ...

Students! We can't hear you. Speak up! Louder, Pia!

Pallavi Keep quiet you guys, let her talk. Go on, Pia.

mangy: looking dirty, uncared for or ill

giggles: laughter

inaudibly: in a voice that cannot be heard

Pia I have a ... (*takes a deep breath now, the decision is taken, then she speaks up*) a monkey!

Class erupts with excitement.

Students Oh! A monkey? Gosh, that's so cool. She's so lucky.

General expressions of admiration and envy.

Teacher Children, children, let her speak. Go on, Pia.

Pia Okay, that's it, I've got a monkey. So, can I go now?

Student 5 Come on, tell us some more.

Teacher Yes, Pia, what a lovely, unusual pet. Do tell us more about it.

Student 1 What's his name?

Pia Er ... (*Waving up a bit of paper that she has in her hand*) Paper ... I mean, Pepper![1]

Student 2 Is it a boy or a girl?

Literary term

1. This is a **pun**. It plays on similar sounding words, **paper** and **pepper**.

Pia A ... girl, definitely a girl.

Student 3 Is it one of those brown monkeys that *bandarwalas* have?

Pia No, it is, it is a ... a Capuchin monkey!

All What?

Pia (*Warming upto her subject now*) A Capuchin monkey. It's a South American breed, it's quite rare.

Student 4 Where did you get it?

Pia My uncle bought her in Chile. He is an animal specialist and so he got her.

Did You Know? **Science**

The word 'capuchin' means hooded. Capuchin monkeys are so named because their white faces, dark brown coat and the fur cover on their head make them look like Spanish Capuchin monks.

Students Wow! How old is she? How long have you had her? What does she eat? What does she wear? Where does she sleep?

Teacher! Children, children, calm down. Calm down please, otherwise I'll have to give you written work!

At this, they immediately quieten down.

Teacher Pia, you've created such a sensation with your monkey. Now, I think the students are not going to be able to concentrate on anything else. A monkey, and that too such a rare **breed.** Why don't you give us a talk ...

breed: (here) belonging to a particular family of animals

stunned: extremely surprised

The bell rings.

Teacher For the next class, Pia, you can prepare a lecture about your very special pet.

Student 5 Yeah, get some photos.

Student 6 Why photos? Why can't Pia bring the monkey to class?

A moment of silence. Pia is very afraid. The others are ***stunned*** *at the brilliance of the idea. Then everyone starts yelling.*

Students Ma'am, tell her to bring the monkey to class!
Yeah, like a 'show and tell', please ma'am. Bring the monkey to class, Pia?

Teacher Alright, alright, I'll ask the Principal for special permission.

The teacher exits and the children crowd around Pia. The class dissolves and the students are now out in the hall. Other children enter the hall from other classes. Pia's classmates run to them and tell them the hot news of the day. Pia stands in her corner and looks at them.

Comprehension

Quick Recap

A. Answer the questions in a few lines.

1. Why were the children in no mood to study that day?
2. Describe Pallavi's character. In what way was her character different from her teacher's?
3. Why was Pia referred to as an 'animal expert'? Why did she make up a story about her pet?
4. Why did the children urge Pia to bring her pet to the class?

B. Read these lines from the play and answer the questions.

1. *'Ma'am look they are stealing my things.'*
   a. Who said this and to whom?
   b. Who are being referred to as 'they' here?
   c. What were they stealing from the speaker?
2. *'Yeah, as most of the lucky ones who've been to my house know, I've got a hutch full of rare angora rabbits.'*
   a. Who said this?
   b. Who was the speaker talking to?
   c. What is the fur of the rabbits used for?

Life Skills and Values imagination, honesty

Think and answer.

1. Do you think Pia did the right thing by making up a story about her pet?
2. Did Pia's actual choice in pets live up to her image as an animal expert?
3. What do you think Pia's feelings were when asked to bring her monkey to the school?

21st Century Critical Thinking

Way with Words

An **idiom** is a group of words which have a different meaning from the meanings of the words it is made of.

Example: Immediately, the class is rocked by **a storm of protests**. (=people expressing their feelings loudly against a situation)

A. Match these animal idioms to their meanings.

Idioms	Meanings
1. cat nap	a. very hot days
2. chicken out	b. a person who does the same thing as someone else
3. rule the roost	c. to decide not to do something out of fear
4. copy cat	d. detect something suspicious
5. dog days	e. make all the decisions in a group
6. smell a rat	f. a short sleep
7. lion's share	g. largest share

B. Now, make sentences with these idioms.

Grammar in Use

Question Tags

Question tags are short questions that come at the end of sentences.

Examples: Art is such great fun, *isn't it*?
She enjoys reading, *doesn't she*?
You are not hungry, *are you*?

The question tag is negative if the statement before it is positive and positive if the statement before it is negative. The question tag uses the same verb as the one in the main sentence.

A. Complete the sentences using the correct question tags.

1. We're late again, ______________?
2. It is quite hot today, ______________?
3. They are leaving for Bengaluru tomorrow, ______________?
4. She is wearing a pretty dress, ______________?
5. We should go to the doctor now, ______________?
6. You live near the Mumbai Sea Link, ______________?
7. He is quite handsome, ______________?

Types of Adverbs

There are four main types of adverbs. These are adverbs of manner, place, time and degree.

An **adverb of place** tells us about the location where the action is taking place. It answers the question *where*?.

Examples: My friend's house is **nearby**. The cat is hiding **under** the bed.

Adverbs of manner describe how, or in what manner, something happens.

Examples: The boy ran **slowly**. He **quickly** agreed to take up the new job.

Adverbs of degree tell us about the intensity or degree of a verb, an adjective or another adverb.

Examples: The water was **extremely** hot. He has **almost** finished his work.

Adverbs of time tell us when an action happened.

Examples: I went to Mumbai **yesterday**. Let's have our sandwiches **now**.

B. Underline the adverbs and state their kind.

1. The girl sweetly sang a Dogri song.
2. The children are playing outside.
3. He plays the piano every Wednesday.
4. My grandmother was walking slowly.
5. The troupe of dancers danced gracefully.
6. She has travelled everywhere.
7. My friend eats extremely slowly.

C. Fill in the blanks with suitable adverbs.

1. It is ____________ cold today. (adverb of degree)
2. Dinner will be served ____________ tonight. (adverb of time)
3. The convocation was held ____________. (adverb of place)
4. Akbar was ____________ pleased to see his favourite courtier, Birbal, again. (adverb of degree)
5. The mother looked at her child ____________. (adverb of manner)
6. I met him ____________ at the function. (adverb of time)
7. The soldiers marched ____________. (adverb of manner)
8. Wait ____________. (adverb of place)

Study Skills

Pronounce Well

Words with Letter 'Q'

The letter **q** can produce two sounds based on its position and its surrounding letters.

- Usually, **'qu'** is pronounced like 'ku'. **Example:** quake
- Sometimes, **'qu'** is pronounced like 'k'. **Example:** mosque

Divide the words in the box according to the pronunciations of 'q'.

question	quick	cheque	quote	boutique	inquest
require	liquid	sequel	oblique	queue	critique

Listening and Speaking

Listen to some funny questions and their witty and intelligent answers. Then, answer the following questions.

1. How do bees get to school?
2. What is a B.?
3. Who gives spoiled milk?
4. Why did the lion feel funny?
5. Which fish swims at night?

Pen it Down

Imagine that you have received a parrot from your uncle as a birthday present. Write an email to your friend describing your new pet. Tell him who gave it to you, where you have kept it, what it looks like, and its habits.

Self Assessment

Now I can

- read and enjoy a play about a girl who makes up a fictional pet.
- practise adverbs and question tags.
- match meanings of some common idioms and write an email.

Read More

The Open Window: This short story by H. H. Munro has a young lady with a gift for making up stories as its central character. It is a story about what happens when someone goes to meet her aunt.

Daddy Long Legs: In this story, Jean Webster tells the tale of an eighteen-year-old girl who has lived all her life in an orphanage. One day, she is told that an unknown person has agreed to pay for her education.

Community and Neighbourhood

17 Pepper, the Phantom Pet–II

Paro Anand

Let's Get Started

Telling truth from fantasy can be tricky. Sometimes it is okay to pretend, but at most times, it is important for us to tell the truth.

Play this fun game in class with the help of your teacher.

- Students will take a sheet of paper. They will write their name on the sheet.
- Next, each student will write something about himself/herself that nobody else in the class knows about them.
- Now, the teacher will call out the names of any five students, but one out of the five will be the person to whom the card belongs.
- The teacher will then read out the statement on the paper.
- All five students will take turns to explain and convince others why the card belongs to them. They can also come up with a back story to prove their case.
- The class will then together decide the person to whom the card belongs.
- Finally, the person to whom the card belongs will step forward. The class will then find out if they guessed correctly. The students in class can then take turns to explain the reasons why they chose that person.

HC **Feelings:** Taking responsibility in conflicts

Reading

Pia has told a white lie that has landed her in a tricky situation. Is she able to get out

of it or will she be caught by everyone? Read on to find out.

Classmates Did you hear about Pia's pet?

Children No, what?

Classmates Pia's got this cool monkey for a pet, called Pepper. She's a girl. She's South American. Pia's going to bring her to school.

Student 7 What, what? Pia's going to bring some South American girl to school? Pia, can you introduce me to her?

Student 4 Not a girl, foolish, a monkey.

Student 7 A monkey, whose monkey?

Pia (*To the audience*) I guess you know that there's no monkey. Everyone expected something really exciting from me. I couldn't disappoint them, could I? I had to give them something to talk about, didn't I?

Student Hey Pia, just heard about your cool new pet!

Pia Yeah, you heard, huh?

Student 3 Why didn't you ever tell us before?

Student 4 Yeah, I mean, something like this! I would have told the whole world in a minute.

Student 3 I would tell it in a nanosecond.

Student 4 How come you kept such a huge thing secret?

Pia I was **embarrassed**, I mean, didn't want to show off, you know.

Student 7 How modest. I would have showed off till I was **blue in the face**!

Student 8 You already do, so just keep quiet and let's hear about the monkey.

Pallavi Pia, the Principal's calling you, he wants to see you about something.

Pia What? Why? What have I done?

Pallavi God knows, I'm just carrying the message.

Enter the Principal. Pia goes to him, trembling. Halfway there, she turns in an aside to the audience.

Pia Oh God, do you suppose that he's got to know about my phantom monkey? Now I'm really in trouble. I tell you, all those books that **moralise** and go on and on about not telling a lie are right, I wish I'd read them a bit more carefully and learnt not to

embarrassed: felt shy about something

blue in the face: absolutely tired

moralise: tell what is right and what is wrong

shoot my mouth off: talk too much

primates: members of the most intelligent group of mammals

whips out: takes out suddenly

shoot my mouth off. Now I'm in really big trouble. (*Goes up to the Principal*) G-ggood morning, sir.

Principal Ah yes, Pia, your teacher has just informed me that you have a delightful monkey as a pet. But this is just wonderful. We are studying **primates**, are we not? I think it would be a wonderful idea for you to bring your monkey to school—what did you say her name was, Garam Masala?

Pia P-p-p-pepper.

Principal Ha ha ha, yes, Pepper! Yes, well, as I was saying, I think we must take this rare opportunity and get this monkey to school. Do you think your parents would mind? Ah yes, maybe I should ring them up and get their permission. (***Whips out** his mobile phone*) Now, what is your father's phone number? I'm sure he wouldn't mind ... hm?

Pia (*To the audience*) Oooh, I'm going to be sick. Help me, someone. (*Doubles over holding her stomach*)

Principal Pia, what's wrong with you? Not feeling well, dear? Then I'd really better call your parents. Give me their mobile numbers, I'll ask them about the monkey and then I'll get them to take you home.

Pia (*Immediately straightening up*) No, no, sir. I'm okay, I'm fine. I-I-I'll ask my parents myself, when I get home. About the monkey, I mean.

Principal But, my child, it may be appropriate if I call them.

Pia No, not appropriate at all, sir. You see, they both have very important meetings today, just now, in fact.

Principal Both of them? Right at this very minute?

Pia This very minute, yes sir. Oooh sir, I don't feel good, I think I'll go lie down for a while.

Principal Oh dear, you don't seem well at all. I better get someone, wait, ah, look, there's your brother. He will help us, don't worry now, my dear. Remind me of your brother's name, Pia.

Pia Oh no, no no no sir, don't call him, sir!

Principal Why child, it's your very own brother. See, he'll take you to the sick room, he can call your parents from my mobile and at the same time I can ask about the monkey. Now, isn't that grand? Avik, that's his name. (*Calling out*) Avik, I say, Avik, come here, please.

Avik (*Running up. Other children gather round to see what's happening*) Yes, sir? Anything wrong, sir? Is this sister of mine in trouble again?

Principal No.

Pia Yes.

sensation: great excitement or interest

Avik and others What?

As the Principal reveals the story, Pia slowly sinks to the ground, her head in her hands.

Principal I think your sister is not feeling too well. I don't know what has happened. She seemed fine until I started asking her about your monkey.

Avik Monkey?

Principal I think we'd better call your parents and let Pia rest at home. I think the excitement of talking about your lovely monkey, Garam Masala, has been too much for her.

Avik Garam Masala?

Pallavi Not Garam Masala, sir, Pepper!

Principal Ah yes, Pepper, Garam Masala, same thing, very spicy.

Avik Pepper? I just don't understand what's going on.

Principal Your sister, Pia, has created a **sensation** in school today by telling her class about your pet monkey, Pepper.

Pallavi Avik! Your uncle's a real dude for bringing a monkey all the way from South America for you.

Pia on the ground, lets out a low moan.

Avik looks at everyone, then bends down to his knees and taps Pia on her shoulder.

Avik So, Pepper's gone to your head finally, has he?

Pia *(Nodding)* She.

Avik What?

Pia She … Pepper, the she-monkey, has gone to my head.

*Avik stands up quickly, Pia holds on to his trouser leg, **pleading**.*

Avik Ah, yes, this is what mom and dad were afraid of. When our uncle got us a monkey, our parents were afraid that Pia would not be able to stand the excitement. They said it would drive her **batty**. It finally has, hasn't it Pia?

Pia nods and doesn't say a word, still hanging her head down. Avik is enjoying this.

Avik She can't handle too much happiness.

Principal My, I've never heard of such an **ailment** before. Too much happiness, fancy that! So, shall we send her home to rest?

Avik No, no. I think there would be nothing like a surprise maths test to calm her down, don't you think, Pia?

Pia throws him a dirty look.

Avik You see, the doctor said that the thing to do is to bring down her level of happiness. That's the only way to handle this, sir, believe me. Pia, don't you agree that a tough little maths test would **sober you up** nicely? Ouch! (*As Pia pinches and punches his leg*) Hmm? (*Raises his eyebrows knowingly at Pia. Pia nods.*) Tell sir that that's just what you'd like, please, Pia.

Pia (*Standing up*) Yes, sir, I'd like to take a maths test to feel better and there are one or two other things I'd like to do!

(***Glowers** at her brother*)

Principal A maths test? Why, I've never quite seen that as a form of medicine before! But I really wanted Pia, or you, for that matter, to bring the monkey to school, if that's possible.

pleading: asking for something in an intense or emotional way
batty: slightly crazy
ailment: a minor illness
sober you up: make you calm down
glowers: looks angrily

Avik Impossible!

Students Why? Please, please say yes. Don't be like that, Avik.

Avik No, actually, it's all my silly sister's fault. My parents, knowing that she is so foolish and can't handle any excitement, have sent the poor monkey back to South America. It's illegal to take wild animals out of their **habitat**, you know. My sister and that uncle of hers, I mean ours, were going to be arrested for mistreatment of a wild animal. So, in order to save her, we had to give her up. In fact, even as we speak, she is on a plane back to her home country and home jungle. We couldn't tell Pia about it, otherwise she would have become completely hysterical.

habitat: the place where an animal or plant normally lives

shepherding: guiding

grumbling: complaining

All, including the Principal Oh, that's just too bad! Gosh, imagine, old Pia was going to be arrested!

Avik Yeah, I was kind of hoping that she would be. I wish I could have shipped her back to the South American jungles and kept the monkey, instead.

*The bell rings. The Principal and the teacher start **shepherding** the children towards the wings.*

Principal Well, well, that's the end of that. Too bad, we won't be able to have such an exotic creature visit us. Now come on everyone, back to class.

Avik Bye Pia, enjoy your maths test! See you at home! I think I'm going to enjoy going home today!

*As the children leave, dragging their feet unwillingly and **grumbling**, Pia moves back to her spot.*

Pia Oh well, I guess that ended the best it could. I'm grateful to my brother, of course, for saving me. But I think he could have been a little kinder. I mean, a maths test? That was really mean! I know he's going to blackmail me now and make me give him chocolates from my share and my comics before I've read them and get him water in the middle of the night. (*Sighs deeply*)
But, I guess it serves me right for monkeying around[1]. Ah well, but let me tell you, I sure did love Pepper the Capuchin monkey, even though she existed only for a little while. Maybe I could write a story about her, or a play and maybe become a famous writer some day.

Lights fade, music plays.

Literary term

1. This is an example of a **pun**. 'Monkeying around' means fooling around, while the play is also about a monkey.

About the author

Paro Anand has written 18 books for children and young adults, including plays and short stories. Some of her well-known books are *No Guns at My Son's Funeral*, *I'm not Butter Chicken* and *Wild Child and Other Stories*.

Comprehension

Quick Recap

A. Answer the questions in a few lines.

1. Why was Pia called by the Principal?
2. What did the Principal want to do?
3. Why did Pia start feeling sick?
4. Why did the Principal call Pia's brother to his room?
5. How did Avik help Pia out of the situation?

B. Read these lines from the play and answer the questions.

1. *'Oh no, no no no sir, don't call him!'*
   a. Who said this and to whom?
   b. Who is being referred to as 'him' here?
   c. Why was the speaker against calling that person?

2. *'A maths test! I've never quite seen that as a form of medicine before!'*
   a. Who said this and to whom?
   b. Who suggested this form of medicine? Who was the patient?
   c. Why was a maths test recommended?

Life Skills and Values

finding solutions

Think and answer.

1. Do you think Pia's brother really helped her?
2. Was Pia a daydreamer? Discuss in the context of the story.
3. In your opinion, was Avik cleverer than Pia?

21ST CENTURY Flexibility

Way with Words

Fields of Study

Pia's uncle was an animal specialist. The study of animals is called zoology. There are many fields of study that end with the suffix **-logy**.

A. Match the names of the fields of study with their descriptions.

A	B
1. biology	a. study of the heart
2. oceanology	b. study of the earth's surface
3. cardiology	c. study of living organisms
4. geology	d. study of words and their meanings
5. lexicology	e. study of oceans

Idioms

B. Match the idioms involving body parts with their meanings.

Idioms	Meanings
1. be all ears	a. good luck
2. cry one's heart out	b. relative
3. break a leg	c. wait eagerly to hear about something
4. flesh and blood	d. an early start
5. get cold feet	e. help (someone do something)
6. give someone a hand	f. cry very hard
7. get a head start	g. be nervous just before a big event

C. Now, make sentences with these idioms.

Grammar in Use

Active and Passive Voice

The **active voice** denotes that the subject of the verb is the doer of the action.

Examples: Pia owns a cool monkey named Pepper.
I should call your parents to get their permission.

The **passive voice** denotes that the subject of the verb is the receiver of the action.

Examples: Pepper, the monkey, is owned as a pet by Pia.
Your parents should be called by me to get their permission.

When a sentence is changed from the active form to the passive, the **object** of the active verb becomes the **subject** of the passive verb.

Examples: He'll take you to the sick room. (active voice)
You will be taken to the sick room by him. (passive voice)

A. Circle the doer in each of these sentences in the active voice.

1. My mother is baking a cake.
2. Monkeys like bananas.
3. The cashier in the bank counted the money.
4. The salesman helped the customer.
5. The company plans to hire college graduates.
6. The school annual day function was very successful.
7. The teacher taught us fractions today in Maths class.
8. Rumani slept early last evening.

B. Change these sentences from the active voice to the passive.

1. Many people speak French in Europe.
2. The government is planning to build a new school in my neighbourhood.
3. Somebody should clean up the room.
4. My father bought a car today.
5. The king and the queen gave a reward to the witty man.
6. I finished all my school work before the match started.
7. My uncle has written three books.
8. My neighbours help the people in the locality.

Study Skills

Spell Check

A. Complete the following words using -ible or -able.

1. accept ____________
2. flex ____________
3. irrespons ____________
4. afford ____________

5. break ____________

6. poss ____________

7. terr ____________

8. favour ____________

Listening and Speaking

In the play, the children and their teacher wanted Pia to bring her pet monkey to school. Do you think this was correct?

Form two groups in class. Hold a debate on the following topic:

Should students be allowed to bring their pets to school?

One group will speak for the motion and the other group will speak against the motion. Each student can speak for three minutes. Students from the opposing team should listen carefully and then be given one minute for asking questions.

Pen it Down

Imagine that Pia actually had a pet monkey at home and the Principal asks her to bring the monkey to school.

Write dialogues for the conversation between Pia and her parents.

You can use the following points:

- Pia's father objects at first
- her mother convinces her father
- Pia is delighted to get permission

Self Assessment

Now I can

- read the final part of the play about what happens to Pia and her 'pet'.
- identify idioms, recognize different fields of study and debate on a given topic.
- practise writing in active and passive voice and write the dialogues of a conversation.

Read More

Dogs Don't Talk: This story by Nancy May is about sixteen-year-old Benjamin McDowell. Benjamin is having a tough time, both at home and school.

Ratatouille: This is a book adaptation by Kitty Richards of the animated film of the same name about Remy, a rat. This is the story of how Remy helps a chef prepare the best dishes in Paris.

Be Creative!

A. 'An Old Friend' is a story set in West Bengal.

Form pairs. Each pair will represent a state of India and design a one-week tour of their state.

You can include the following points:

- the best season for going there
- places to explore
- things to eat

Both the students forming the pair must speak. You can also draw pictures or do charades to demonstrate the major attractions of the tour.

B. Imagine that you work at a local radio station and are reporting on the fire at Presamber Grance in the story, 'Shall We Ghost?'. Form groups of five. One student is to be the news reader, one the interviewer and the other three the people who are being interviewed. The news reader in each group will present the introduction and the conclusion. The interviewer will ask questions.

Some sample questions can be:

- Who do you think was responsible for the strange happenings?
- Which incident stands out in your memory as being the funniest?
- Did you feel scared?

C. Divide the class into two groups - Group A and Group B. Each student will tell the members of his/her group an adjective that best describes him/her.

Now, students of Group A will describe each of the members. They will not take the described person's name. Group B has to guess the name of the student. After Group A, Group B will describe its members and Group A has to guess. The team with the most number of correct guesses wins.

D. Pia made up a story in class about Pepper, her pet. As a result, she had to be saved by her brother and had to sit for a maths test.

Match the cause to the effect.

Cause	Effect
1. The car jumped a red light. •	• a. She was hungry before lunch.
2. Benu stayed up late. •	• b. She was sleepy in school.
3. The students were quiet in class. •	• c. The students got wet.
4. It rained after school. •	• d. The teacher gave them a reward.
5. Lavina skipped breakfast. •	• e. Another car hit it.

Literary Genres and Terms

Literary Genres

The reading texts which you have read in this book are of various types. The following are some common types of stories, poems and plays.

Prose

An **adventure** is a type of story or book which has a lot of action, danger, risk and excitement.

A **fable** is a story with a moral lesson at the end. In fables, animals, plants and non-living things often speak like humans.

A **fairy tale** is a story which has magical events and creatures like fairies, elves and goblins.

Light verse is humorous poetry, usually dealing with playful themes and aimed at amusing the reader.

A **descriptive poem** describes in detail the subject of the poem rather than telling a story or talking about feelings.

A **short story** narrates a tale that is only a few pages long.

Non-fiction is a type of prose that is based on real events rather than imaginary ones.

A **folktale** is a story common among people who come from the same background. It is usually passed on in the form of an oral tale.

A **biography** is a book about a famous person and their life events written by another person.

A **graphic story** is a story told through words and pictures arranged in a sequence, with dialogues given in speech bubbles.

An **autobiography** is a type of story or book in which the author writes about stories and events from his/her own life.

Poetry

A **lyric poem** is a short poem whose main purpose is to express emotions or a state of mind. It does not depict actions or events, as narrative poems do.

A **nonsense poem** is a light-hearted, rhyming poem, often for young people, with peculiar characters in unusual situations or an unusual way of describing everyday things.

A **ballad** is a narrative poem that tells a story through dialogue and actions and is often set to music. They were originally written for dances.

A **comedy** is a play with a light or humorous tone where the characters overcome difficult circumstances in the end. A comedy may not always be about amusing people or incidents.

Literary Terms

Literary terms include common figures of speech. These are the various techniques writers use to convey their message.

A **simile** is a figure of speech in which someone or something is compared to a very different person or thing using 'as' or 'like'. **Example:** He is as brave as a lion.

A **metaphor** is a figure of speech in which a person or thing is compared to another, otherwise unrelated person or thing by stating that they are the same in a particular way. **Example:** She is a rose.

Personification is a way of imagining non-living things or abstract ideas as human beings with thoughts, actions and emotions. **Example:** The moon danced over the water.

Alliteration is a figure of speech in which the same consonant sound is repeated in consecutive or closely placed words in the same sentence. **Example:** Slithering snakes slither silently through the grass.

Onomatopoeia is the use of words whose pronunciation is similar to the sounds they represent. **Examples:** honk, bang, buzz.

Exclamation is a figure of speech which is used to draw attention to something in a way that a simple statement cannot. It is used to express surprise, strong emotion or pain. **Example:** How tall the mountain is!

A **pun** is a literary device which plays on the different meanings of the same word, or the similar sound of different words, to produce a humorous effect. **Example:** Without geometry, life is pointless.

Repetition is a literary device where the same word or phrase is repeated at intervals to give stress on a particular idea. **Example:** But I have promises to keep, /And miles to go before I sleep, /And miles to go before I sleep.

A **hyperbole** is a figure of speech in which the writer exaggerates and makes something sound bigger or more impressive than it really is. **Example:** 'I told you a thousand times!'